The Practice Process

Revolutionise practice to maximise enjoyment, motivation and progress

Paul Harris

FABER ff MUSIC

© 2014 by Paul Harris
First published in 2014 by Faber Music Ltd
All rights administered worldwide by Faber Music Ltd
Bloomsbury House
74–77 Great Russell Street
London WC1B 3DA
Text and cover design by Susan Clarke
Printed in England by Caligraving Ltd

ISBN10: 0-571-53833-9
EAN13: 978-0-571-53833-1

To buy Faber Music publications or to find out about the full range of titles available
please contact your local music retailer or Faber Music sales enquiries:
Faber Music Ltd, Burnt Mill, Elizabeth Way, Harlow CM20 2HX
Tel: +44 (0) 1279 82 89 82   Fax: +44 (0) 1279 82 89 83
sales@fabermusic.com   fabermusic.com

Contents

Acknowledgments

I would like to dedicate this book to the memory of a truly great teacher: Professor John Davies, who taught me to play and practise from the age of nine and ever after remained a mentor, continually supporting and challenging my thinking. For all his many students – among whom number principals of music colleges, world-renowned conductors and many world-class teachers and players – his most enduring ability was to instil a sense of self-belief, a humble confidence and a gentle dignity. These are the qualities we need to instil in our pupils as we take them into a very new age of practice.

I've also been very fortunate to have studied with other inspirational teachers and to know and work with many wonderful teachers too. Many have read this manuscript and shared their thoughts on this highly fascinating and emotive subject. Here they are, and to all, huge thanks.

Sally Adams, Catherine Black, Liz Childs, Jean Cockburn, Richard Crozier, Sezil Güler, Pat Hayler, Diana Jackson, Brian Ley, Helen Leek, Isabel Matson, Julia Middleton, Leonie Minty, Ann Priestley, Francesca Rogers, Alan Taylor, Robert Tucker, Simon Walker and Hector Wells. Many thanks also to the superb team at Faber Music: Richard King, Kathryn Knight, Phil Jarvis and my exceptional editor, Lesley Rutherford, whose support and unfailing positivity has made it all possible.

Who the book is for

Although written primarily for teachers, both parents and pupils will learn a lot from it too.

A few words about *practice* (or *practise*)

In this instance, I mean the word: how *do* you spell it? In the USA they have solved the problem and spell both the noun and the verb in the same way. How *very* sensible! Here in the UK we insist on maintaining different spellings for noun and verb. If, like me, you don't always get it right, may I suggest the trick of simply replacing it (temporarily that is) with either advice (the noun) or advise (the verb) to see if you have made the appropriate choice.

Forewords

'I find this an inspiring and, may I say, revolutionary approach to this tricky subject. Practice is such an important topic and you have drilled it to the core. Your approach is revolutionary but also a natural progression from your previous work and philosophy: your suggestions for practice really are innovative though in many ways quite obvious. Empowerment, motivation and independent learning are key principles – all of which provide a foundation for meaningful and profitable practice during the time each week that pupils are not with us. This book provides so many answers and gives so many ideas: you have not only introduced a new approach to practice but you have also shared so many tips and ideas to help teachers put practice into practice!'

Brian Ley, former music adviser, inspector and consultant

'It is so refreshing to read your books – I do so with a smile on my face as you just hit the spot. I do believe that your books should be compulsory reading for all those downtrodden teachers who don't have any connection with their peers or find any joy in their teaching.'

Diane Widdison, Musicians' Union National Organiser, Education and Training

'As a music teacher, *The Practise Process* has rejuvenated my teaching. My students have embraced the opportunity to be *empowered* to practise rather than pressed to do so. The 'to do' list is no more, replaced by a collaborative process, resulting in many students starting journeys of independent learning, creativity and critical thinking. It has been a joy to watch children blossom and develop in their musical learning with wonderful compositions written, improvisations played, composers discovered and scales actually learnt! The benefits are two way, I have learnt from my students. The 21st century child is more autonomous than ever, embracing the opportunity to be a 'partner' in their practice programmes. Bravo Paul: as always, you show us a way to walk around the side of the mountain instead of having to go over the top of it. My students and their parents are very grateful, as am I: you have expanded my thinking yet again!'

Karen Marshall, teacher

'...In *The Practice Process* you are right in the stream of research and thinking about effective formative assessment, next-step marking and enabling the child to own their learning journey – all disciplines from the classroom which you are translating, applying and extending into music teaching and learning. You do this in a way that feels intuitive rather than artificial and theoretical: 'Ah yes, of course, why aren't I doing that already?' In particular I love the practice map (visual!), the integration with life, the way you integrate the psychological with the technical and social, and the many ideas and suggestions you generate. You, like me, believe in the power of pupil self-assessment, pupil's metacognitive development and teacher-pupil dialogue. Thanks again for allowing me to read your book.'

Simon Walker, Director, Human Ecology Education

'*The Practice Process* combines real insight, understanding and experience with humour and sympathy. This book has encouraged me to question and reassess my values, judgements and motivations in relation to practice, which will contribute to my personal development as both a player and a teacher.'

Leonie Minty, student and teacher

1 'My tortoise had a headache ...'

Practice is a place. It is a place where those learning music should want to visit frequently. It's going to be up to us to make that place somewhere our pupils want to go. That's what this book is about.

A number of our pupils may practise with pleasure. For all the rest (and, let's face it, that's probably quite a percentage) we have to find the key that opens the rather stiff and heavy door into that fascinating land we call practice. If we can help them to open that door, once through it and given the right directions, pupils will find practice a much more friendly and hospitable place than they may have first thought.

As you're probably aware, there are a good number of books and articles on the subject of practice. I have read many of them and I've visited a good deal of the numerous internet sites that reflect on the subject too. Most tell us *how* to practise; many tell us *what* to practise; some discuss how we should *approach* practice. But even with all this easily accessible and worthy advice on the subject (and some of it has been available for a long time), a great many of our pupils *still* don't seem to like doing any. Many of them may do a little (though often reluctantly), and quite a number don't do any at all. They do however seem keen and able to engage their imaginations when presenting their excuses. Here are some particularly memorable ones:

> *'The dog ate my music.'*
>
> *'The piano is under dust sheets.'*
>
> *'I couldn't find my tuba!'*
>
> *'My dad left some important papers on the piano lid which I wasn't allowed to move.'*
>
> This next one I've never quite worked out:
> *'My sister got a new pair of shoes.'*
>
> And my all-time favourite:
> *'My tortoise had a headache ...'*

I'm sure you have your own favourites to add to this list of genuine excuses collected from teacher-friends. If only our pupils were as imaginative in actually *doing* their practice as they were in inventing these wonderful reasons to explain why they *didn't* do any.

If you have dutiful pupils who don't find it necessary to make excuses, but instead practise regularly, effectively, without having to be nagged and in a positive, well-directed and enthusiastic frame of mind, then this book is probably not for you. If, on the other hand, your pupils are more resourceful in thinking up reasons for not practising than they are when considering what to do during practice, then read on! Join me on a journey that will demystify and explore this complex, sensitive and vital part of our teaching.

Spoilt for choice

Young people today have a wealth of activities that they can choose from to fill their time. If practising is to be one of them, then we need to make it desirable and something they actually *want* to do. If we don't, then most of them won't do any. Let's not pretend otherwise.

The reality is that many aspiring young musicians (including some of our advanced pupils and even a number of professionals) find settling down to practise a real challenge; which is quite understandable given the instant gratification of so many alternative, and often highly attractive, activities. Add to that the considerable mental and physical effort that practising requires and we have a dilemma.

We need, therefore, to give a lot of thought to practice and how to entice our pupils, willingly and enthusiastically, into it. So this is a book *about* practice. It's about how teachers and parents serve up and manage practice. The intention is to develop a more psychological and holistic approach: how to set up the best *mental* environment for getting pupils to practise. We will try to discover strategies and structures to motivate our pupils to do some (eagerly) and to enjoy the experience! En route, we will examine and explore why it is that practice can cause anxiety and stress for so many. And in trying to understand our pupils' worries, doubts and fears, we will begin to unlock the secrets of generating positive practice.

Unlike so many other books on the subject, this is not essentially a *what-to-practise* or a *how-to-practise* book. There won't be many tips on how to play semiquaver patterns more evenly or how to remember the notes that make up an arpeggio of C sharp minor (though one or two ideas may creep in along the way). But it will help us understand why so many pupils often find these very things so difficult to do and how we can help them to find a way forward. It's a book about creating a positive mindset towards this hugely valuable and potentially deeply enjoyable activity that seems to have earned itself so much bad press over the years.

Let's see whether we can open that door, creating and inspiring a new generation of pupils who positively can't wait to get practising!

2 The revolution starts here!

'So what have you been practising this week?'

It's a fair question. And here's what might happen in a perfect world:

> If the week's practice was set up with considerable care ... If our pupil really understood the prescribed activities and all the various ingredients involved ... If, during the actual practice, our pupil felt a sense of achievement and understood how it fitted into an enjoyable and meaningful ongoing learning programme ... And if our pupil knows that whatever has been practised will be duly acknowledged and will form the basis for the next lesson ...

... then we might expect the answer to be enthusiastic, informative and filled with a positive eagerness for the ensuing lesson.

But the truth is (if the answer is indeed truthful) that the question is more likely to be met with a rather negative and defensive response:

> *'I haven't had time to do much ...'*
>
> *'I only had time this week to go through my piece last night and it didn't go very well.'*
>
> *'I couldn't remember the notes of C sharp minor arpeggio and got annoyed.'*
>
> *'I didn't really understand what you wanted me to do and besides, I was too busy.'*

Pupils, from time immemorial, have found endless reasons for not practising. In Chapter 4 we'll look at why. But right now I'd like to suggest a method through which we can get our pupils to change their attitude and begin to think much more positively and enthusiastically about their practice.

The three prongs of productive practice

If practice is delivered as a sort of 'bolt-on' at the end of a lesson, we certainly can't be confident that it will be done enthusiastically, or indeed at all! We need to find a method whereby it becomes a natural extension of the lesson and will always be carried out with purpose and pleasure.

We probably do have one group of pupils who practise with pleasure – and it's usually more than just pleasure: this group frequently really love it. I'm thinking of our beginners. It's all new and exciting and they often can't get enough of it. But for many, that euphoria soon begins to fade as the novelty wears off, progress seems to slow down and everything becomes more complicated.

What goes wrong? How can we retain this enthusiasm?

The whole problem has largely arisen because we have the notion that the success of our pupils' practice is mostly because of things that *they* do rather than things that *we* do. If our part in their practising process is simply giving them a list of things to do, it's highly likely that things will not be done. If we're going to start a real transformation, a practice revolution, we are going to have to take on more responsibility and begin to manage their practice with more care. This doesn't necessarily mean more work or a seismic shift in what we already do. But it will require a change of approach.

The difference is that this new approach puts practice *centre stage* in our teaching and allows pupils to see it as a natural part of a vibrant, ongoing and organic process, rather than an often tedious and only vaguely related optional extra.

The basis of this approach is really very straightforward and simply requires us to make sure that three things happen. To some extent, we're probably doing them already – it will just be a case of refining and managing them more effectively.

- The first is that we *regularly* talk about, explain, discuss and describe the practice that our pupils are going to do, during the *whole course of the lesson*.
- The second is that we decide and set down what is to be done in collaboration with our pupils, and *in a very clear, understandable and engaging manner*. It's not a question of telling our pupils what they are to practise. The actual substance of a week's practice needs to develop as a result of a dialogue with them and it needs to be set out with imagination.
- The third is that we assiduously generate each new lesson out of the practice that pupils have done.

So, in three words:

Integration, Representation and Connection

I call this the *Simultaneous Practice Cycle*. Let's have a closer look at how works and the ways in which we can develop our present strategies to ge it going.

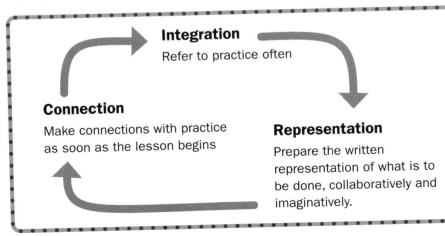

Integration
Refer to practice often

Connection
Make connections with practice as soon as the lesson begins

Representation
Prepare the written representation of what is to be done, collaboratively and imaginatively.

Integration – Representation – Connection

Transformation No.1 **Integration**: refer to practice often.

It's as simple as that. As a lesson develops we need to integrate talking about and referring to practice regularly. Try to use the following kind of questions and comments frequently:

> *'What would you like to practise?'*
>
> *'What do you think is important to practise here?'*
>
> *'When you practise this ...'*
>
> *'Are you clear about how to practise that?'*
>
> *'Which connection will you make first?'*
>
> *'How might you practise this?'*
>
> *'I think you'll really enjoy practising ...'*
>
> *'Do you think you'll need to practise this? How will you do it?'*
>
> *'How much of this piece would you like to work on?'*
>
> *'What will you think about when practising this?'*
>
> *'Could you tell me how you're going to practise that?'*
>
> *'What will be your first thought when you begin practising?'*

In a way the *primary function* of a lesson is to set up the week's practice – especially if we'd like some to be done! As we continually integrate practice in this way, two very important things are happening in our pupils' minds. Firstly they are learning to feel comfortable with the idea, and secondly we are beginning to develop their confidence and appetite to engage willingly and enthusiastically with it. We are personalising it and making it feel friendly. The *concept* of practice begins to feel warmer, cosier and more secure rather than cold, distant and perhaps threatening – the sort of place so many pupils currently associate with practice. Listen to your tone of voice, too, when discussing practice – it should always be warm, encouraging and sincere. From lesson one onwards practice must be delivered as a natural and pleasant *extension* of the lesson.

Integration – *Representation* – Connection

Transformation No 2 **Representation**: prepare the written representation of what is to be done, collaboratively and imaginatively.

How do we usually indicate what pupils are to practise? Perhaps we make a list in our pupils' notebooks, or in one of those special practice books that come with inviting cartoons on the cover. Perhaps we simply tick pieces in their book. And when do we scribble down these requests? Usually at the end of the lesson when the time is running out fast ...

Do pupils take much notice of these often barely decipherable invitations to work at this technical point, practise such and such a piece or song and work at these (probably unrelated) scales?

Perhaps I'm being a little unfair – many teachers do take a lot of trouble over their practice wish list. Even so, many pupils still take little notice. In regular conversations I've had with young learners, the number who admit to ignoring their teachers' practice suggestions is disturbingly high.

If we are to engage the maximum number of pupils in the most effective practice, we need to move away from the end-of-the-lesson list and find an alternative that will attract the imagination, cause pupils to look forward to practising and help them really develop their playing or singing.

The answer to that alternative lies in embracing the knowledge that brains are organic rather than linear learning devices. Instead of 'the list', we need to show pupils how the various elements connect. How, when practising, pupils can flow easily and knowingly from one element to another, *always achieving* and developing true understanding and confidence. This really is very important – too often the effort that pupils put in to practice shows little benefit and there are few (or indeed no) rewards: a process destined for failure. **Pupils must see and understand the rewards of their work if we are to turn practice into a positive experience.**

If you are a Simultaneous Learning teacher[1] you will know how important it is to teach through making relevant connections, all the time showing pupils how those connections fit into the bigger picture, and travelling through each lesson by building on existing skills and understanding. This is how you need to proceed within the practice environment, so to this end I have devised the **Simultaneous Learning Practice Map**. Instead of a list, we can map the areas and activities for practice in a visual way so that pupils really see the relevance of what they are doing and how it all connects. Additionally, the great advantage of the Practice Map is that we generate it *during* the lesson (not at the end) and always in collaboration with our pupils. We'll go into detail on exactly how to use the Practice Map in the next chapter.

Integration – Representation – *Connection*

> Transformation No.3 **Connection**: make connections with practice as soon as the new lesson begins.

The third prong of the Simultaneous Practice Cycle is making meaningful and clear connections with what has been practised, *at the beginning of the lesson*. Whilst teachers do usually draw on what their pupils may have practised at some point in the lesson, if we are to make a real difference, we must make that connection *right away*. This demonstrates to pupils the considerable importance we attach to their practice (whatever they managed to do) and how it will constitute the basis of their ongoing learning process. I have seen so many lessons where pupils' practice was only alluded to, almost in passing, or was even taken for granted. Neither approach will strengthen pupils' relationship with practice.

Talk to pupils about what they actually did and ensure there is lots of praise for their choices, the connections they made, the effort they put in and the strategies used as well as their achievements. In fact, giving pupils the chance

to talk about their recent practice and offering positive and const[...]
feedback and appreciation in such close proximity to their work is the *lifebl[...]
of this method*. This conversation has to occur when pupils are most intereste[...]
and can make the best use of the feedback.

> So, in summary, we need to make three transformations:
> • In the lesson, refer to practice a lot more often.
> • Make the written representation of practice imaginative, engaging, and very much in collaboration with the pupil.
> • Make connections with practice as soon as the lesson begins.

Not massive, but massively significant. Put the Simultaneous Practice Cycle into motion and watch how self-motivation and self-responsibility begin to grow.

'So what *have* you been practising this week?'

Over time, and if we really get into the flow, this question will begin to be treated seriously. Pupils will grow in their deep understanding of how the whole process works. Their practice ceases to be a remote or disconnected activity – it is acknowledged as a major part of their learning. They know that the first thing the teacher will ask is what they have practised – not to find out whether they did any, but because it will play a vital role in what happens next. It is then up to us to accept, unconditionally for the most part, whatever the answer is.

> *'I just practised the first note of this piece – working on sound quality and expression.'*
>
> *'I've been exploring and connecting all the ingredients in this piece.'*
>
> *'I worked on the first two notes of the C sharp minor arpeggio.'*
>
> *'I've been working on an improvisation based on the ingredients from my new song.'*
>
> *'I've been working on the whole first movement of this sonata.'*
>
> *'I've been experimenting with staccato.'*

Whatever the answer, we take it (or part of it) as the starting point of our lesson: our Simultaneous Learning warm-ups. It is always our pupils who will determine the initial direction of the lesson. They will soon begin to understand their fundamental importance in the teaching/learning process. Allow the process to develop naturally and don't be in a hurry for the penny to drop. It will eventually, and you will have begun to develop pupils for whom the concept of practice is seen as a natural and approachable extension of the lesson.

As this method becomes more and more familiar, we will begin to notice a momentum building up, a flow of energy that will really enthuse our pupils – and, in turn, ourselves.

Simultaneous Learning

I devised Simultaneous Learning as an entirely positive, non-judgmental and imaginative way to teach. Through this method, we move far away from the tedious and negative form of teaching that spends most of its time reacting to poor work, mistakes and a general lack of real understanding. It is based on an approach that takes into account the fact that the brain is an organic, not linear, learning device. It embraces the understanding that all the elements of music are connected. It sets up a positive energy and a positive learning environment that really motivates pupils because they are always achieving and understanding. I have written about it extensively in *Improve Your Teaching!*, *Teaching Beginners* and *The Virtuoso Teacher*.

Here is a brief introduction for those who are not familiar with it. It is based on three principles:

Teach pro-actively

To begin, we set up short, single-focussed *sequential* activities – each one leading to and from something the pupil can do. The pupil is therefore always achieving and building up a broader understanding of how everything fits together. Learning and skill building become enjoyable, imaginative and positive, and the process becomes an exciting voyage of discovery.

As the understanding of a piece's ingredients and musical concepts becomes clear, we can then move on to setting up (still pro-actively) longer sections or passages – four bars, half a piece and eventually a whole piece. We *will* 'react' (as we did in the shorter activities) but always to well-prepared work. Our response can then be affirmative, suggesting refinements and more single-focussed work where necessary. Simultaneous Learning is energising for both pupil and teacher. Mistakes are few and far between (pupils will generally know if they make one and will be able to deal with the problem creatively). Pupils are always motivated.

Teach from the ingredients

We identify and work at various ingredients in the piece or song being learned (the key, scale, character, rhythmic patterns, markings, etc.) through short improvisation and imaginative exercises and then ...

... make connections

We move forward (through these short sequential activities) by making appropriate connections using the chosen ingredients. Perhaps we begin with the key of the piece and connect with the scale ... then the scale with a rhythm from the piece ... the rhythm with some aural ... aural with some theory ... theory with some sight-reading ... sight reading with some improvisation. Then back to another aspect of the piece for the next Simultaneous Learning journey.

By working with our pupils around the 'map' of learning, they really understand how it all fits together.[2]

2 Of course, everything connects to everything, but the map gives a good general impression.

The Simultaneous Learning map

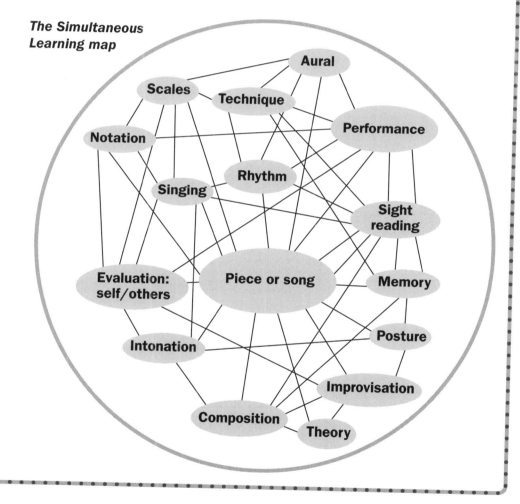

3 The Simultaneous Learning Practice Map

When things go seriously wrong

We're sending a pupil home to do a first practice on a new piece or song. What so often happens, unless that pupil *really* knows and understands all the ingredients, is that he/she returns the next week with anything from a few mistakes to a whole raft of them. If the pupil dutifully 'practised' a number of times, many of these mistakes will have developed deep roots which makes our job of correcting them all the more difficult. So straight away, at the start of the next lesson, we're into the most negative kind of reactive teaching: correcting mistakes. And there's nothing much we can do about it. All our desires to give a positive, pro-active, Simultaneous Learning lesson have to be suspended; our general desire to be a positive, pro-active, Simultaneous Learning teacher is thwarted.

Any significant amount of *purely* reacting-to-mistakes type teaching usually results in frustration. So clearly we have a problem here. A problem in which the solution hinges on the way we manage **the first lesson and practice of a new piece**, which makes those two related activities the *most critical of all in our teaching*.

It's essential that we manage the first lesson and practice with enormous care. If we don't, then we're always going to end up in that negative world of mistake correction. If we do, gradually we will ease ourselves into the wholly positive world of Simultaneous Learning; we never need find ourselves anywhere else ever again!

The way we send pupils home to do that first practice on their new piece really is *vital*.

Look carefully at the pieces your pupils are about to take home and work on. Do they really know enough to make their practice entirely positive, so that they can bring the piece back to the next lesson without mistakes? Or is the notation going to produce feelings of anxiety? Is the potential for what we might call 'negative-learning' during practice greater than the potential for 'positive-learning'?

3 For an example, see page 19.

4 See page 15.

5 The *Simultaneous Learning Practice Map Pad* (Faber Music).

The **Simultaneous Learning Practice Map**[3] is an idea that will significantly change the way that we set down our instructions for a pupil's practice. Rather than the traditional list, it is a map formed by laying out brief and concise ideas in bubbles (based on the Simultaneous Learning model diagram[4]). The map has a dual purpose: it represents work done in the lesson and it will guide pupils through their practice. These maps are available to purchase.[5] Let's look at how to use this idea.

The first lesson on a new piece

Here's a scenario in which we are giving the first lesson on this little piece (simply think of it in terms of your own instrument or voice and make the appropriate transposition/clef change, etc.).

Walking to School

It may be, after one lesson, that your pupil really does understand *everything* about this piece and will come back with every detail correct. But that's not usually what happens.

So ... firstly, in customary Simultaneous Learning fashion, let's identify the ingredients:

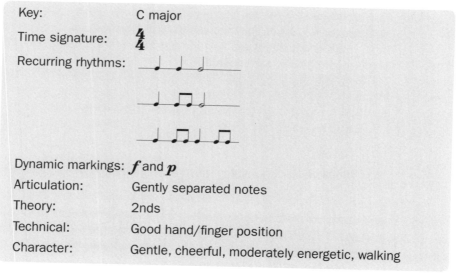

Next, with a Simultaneous Practice Map to hand, we begin to give a Simultaneous Learning lesson working through and making connections between the piece's ingredients. The book is closed – 'the music' itself is out of sight. Simultaneous Learning journeys evolve through pro-actively setting up activities and then moving forward depending on our pupils' response. Here's how our first 'teaching journey' on *Walking to School* might unfold:

Set up a 4/4 pulse at a walking pace and ask the pupil to clap the pulse while you play a continuous melody, using just the notes and rhythms from the piece.

Pupil claps in time, steadily and with a sense of metre.

In the same pulse, try some call and response clapping, using rhythms from the piece.

Pupil claps back in time, accurately and energetically.

Add **p** and **f** to your rhythmic call and responses.

Pupil responds musically, keeping time and with a good ear for contrast.

Using the same pulse, introduce the micro-scale (the first five notes) of C major, with one ♩ per note. Listen to the evenness of tone quality.

Pupil plays back accurately and in time. Small refinements to hand/finger position are made.

Talk briefly about the key and the name of the notes. Perhaps ask the pupil to write the notes down.

Pupil knows the notes and understands the 'key'.

Play the scale again, adding some of the rhythms and the two dynamic levels.

Pupil enjoys combining these ingredients and plays musically.

Improvise, in a walking character, using the ingredients explored so far.

Pupil enjoys improvising and creates interesting music that has an obvious walking character.

As we moved through these activities our pupil was continually engaged, clearly enjoying the process, and growing in confidence. We made connections to many elements of musical learning (pulse and rhythm, aural, sound and dynamics, theory, technique, scales, improvisation, characterisation and memory). And most important of all, there was always a sense of *positive achievement*.

At the end of this series of activities, which took perhaps ten minutes, we put some of these ingredients onto our Practice Map and discuss how they might be practised. It is better to do this at the end of each teaching journey, as we don't want to interrupt the flow. Here's what the filled-in Practice Map might look like:

SIMULTANEOUS LEARNING
PRACTICE MAP

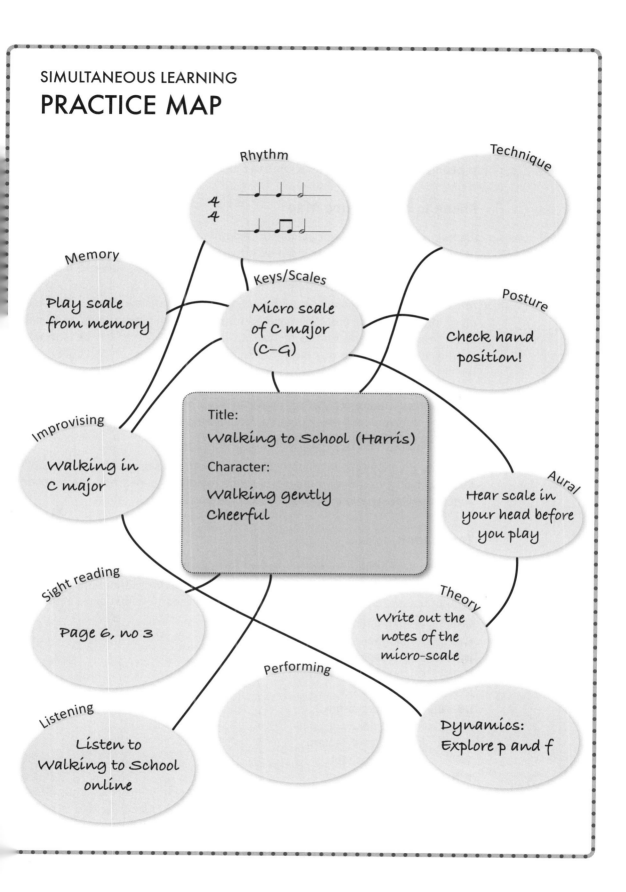

Rhythm

Technique

Memory

Play scale
from memory

Keys/Scales

Micro scale
of C major
(C-G)

Posture

Check hand
position!

Improvising

Walking in
C major

Title:
Walking to School (Harris)

Character:
Walking gently
Cheerful

Aural

Hear scale in
your head before
you play

Sight reading

Page 6, no 3

Theory

Write out the
notes of the
micro-scale

Performing

Listening

Listen to
Walking to School
online

Dynamics:
Explore p and f

Ideally it should be a combination of teacher and pupil who actually fill out the map (why this is better than just the teacher we will discuss in Chapter 6). Because the bubbles are quite small, there is not much space for long-winded instructions or explanations. We must trim everything down to the absolute minimum (which means we're able to express all that we require much more quickly). We simply don't need lots of words if the ideas we are introducing in the lesson (and which form their practice) are appropriate, part of a logical and sequential process and have, as a result, been *clearly understood* by the pupil.

Filling in the Practice Map

We begin with the *title and composer* and some description of the *character*. (Why is it that these elements are so often ignored by learners?) Then, in the appropriate bubbles, we add the ingredients that we have been working on and would like our pupil to continue to explore in practice. We may add a sight-reading piece to be looked at, perhaps on day 3, because we know it's made up of ingredients our pupil will have no trouble processing. We may be aware of an interesting performance of *Walking to School* online which we suggest they watch, perhaps on day 4. In this instance we use the untitled bubble for the dynamic markings, but we might have used it for composing, intonation, articulation, mental practice, a bit of research or anything else that might be important as a result of that particular lesson. We certainly don't need to fill in all the bubbles each week: just the appropriate ones. We then add to them in the next lesson.

Using the Practice Map in group teaching will both save time and focus pupils' thinking. Filling in the map should be done mostly by pupils with the teacher simply overseeing and checking. Keep some pencils handy!

Text-speak

Given the deliberately confined space of each bubble, you and your pupils may like to develop some useful, space-saving and fun abbreviations (much in the style of text-speak). Here are some common phrases to help make a start:

GPP	Good posture, please!
R2R	Remember to relax
R2WU	Remember to do your warm-ups
CWS	Connect with scales!
PLN	Play long notes
DS@B1	Don't start at bar 1
S@B...	Start at bar...
MALS	Make a lovely sound
TAT	Think about tone
HIH	Hear in your head
LTY	Listen to yourself
PWC	Play with character
MUAS	Make up a story
LHO	Left hand only
PS	Practise slowly

PSM	Practise in slow motion
CYI	Clean your instrument!
FOA...	Find out about...
PFM	Play from memory
MLOC	Make lots of connections
SOL	Sing out loud
TW	Technical work
EDy	Explore dynamics
WaM	With a metronome

At home[6]

r wherever
tice takes
e.

So, armed with a Practice Map our pupil sets to, preferably the same day as the lesson, and begins by thinking about what happened in the lesson and about the title of the piece. Then it's the key and scale. Through careful Simultaneous Learning and regular reinforcement, pupils 'get' the concept of the key and the scale (the 'building blocks' of the piece): *That's what we did in the lesson – I understood it and it was fun.'* The pupil plays the micro-scale and then joins the 'Keys/scales' bubble with the 'Title/character' box with a line. We have moved a long way from pupils thinking, *'Here's a boring scale that I have to learn, even though I don't know why – and I can't remember the notes anyway, because I can't see the point.'*

erhaps help the
l with joining
he bubbles
first time you
duce the
tice Map. The
l might like to
o the lines in
ferent colour
ubsequent
tice sessions.

Drawing that line is *hugely significant.*[7] It's a physical action that represents the actual neural connection in the brain between two thoughts – in this case, the piece and the key.

It's then up to pupils to decide which connection they might like to make next – they may choose aural or technique, rhythm or theory. Simply having to think through and make these decisions plays a very powerful part in pupils' learning. So they make the next connection, do the activity and draw another connecting line. And so on ...

In the early stages of learning to practise in the Simultaneous Learning way, it's important that we teach our pupils how to make these decisions. But they'll soon get it. In the world of nature, the most successful are those who make good decisions. In the world of practice, our pupils will soon learn which are the best connections to make, allowing their practice to become more and more effective. And because pupils are taking ownership of the direction of their practice (rather than 'following orders') their self-esteem grows, they are more engaged and learning is really taking place.

Eventually all the bubbles will be joined up (not necessarily in the first practice) and connections and understandings solidly made. In subsequent days, perhaps using a different coloured pen or pencil for each day, pupils might:

- make more connections.
- go over the same connections again, developing them further.
- approach them in a different order, thus reinforcing the understanding of the concepts by coming to them from new angles and making multiple links.
- bring another bubble into play (which becomes increasingly possible as

pupils begin to understand how both the Practice Map and the whole idea of practice works).

It's all engaging, meaningful, relevant, creative and fun. Above all, pupils really are learning. They will be truly embedding these concepts, ideas and skills into their own minds: understanding and (perhaps most importantly) learning to be in full control of their own practice.

The next lesson

Practice is the first thing we talk about in the next lesson. What we do next is entirely dependent on our pupils' responses. As we work out what they did, we might decide:

- to do more activities without the music, either adding more ideas or filling out more bubbles on the original sheet;
- to create a new Practice Map (still working without the notation) developing the same ideas and adding more;
- that the ingredients *are* sufficiently well understood so that we can now introduce the music copy itself and begin a new map with a fresh set of activities, this time based around the notation.

We simply feed whatever pupils have practised into our Simultaneous Learning teaching and we're off on another positive journey.

The *very first* practice ever ... [8]

8 In fact not just the very first, but the first few.

is *extremely* important. If we are lucky enough to start a pupil from scratch, let's take that golden opportunity to ensure that we set practice up to be imaginative and exciting.[9] Using the Simultaneous Learning Practice Map we can introduce appropriate ingredients for the beginner to explore, play with and connect. With the help of a parent, our beginners will use the map to shape their own creative practice journeys – from the first lesson onwards.

9 *Teaching Beginners* (Faber Music) discusses this whole area in detail.

If beginners are simply given a piece to take home and practise (which they certainly will, with much enthusiasm) then they will rapidly form the idea that practising is just *playing through a piece or singing through a song*. We want to give our pupils a very different notion of what practice is all about.

Making the transition – and the 'No Practice' ploy

If you do decide to adopt this method of teaching and practice (either completely or in part) you will have to find ways of bringing pupils round to the new approach. Most will embrace it with enormous enthusiasm and 'get it' immediately. With others you may have to take it a little more slowly. For pupils who generally do more harm than good in their practice (learning endless mistakes whilst playing through their pieces, with brain mostly disengaged) you may like to employ this rather dramatic tactic: **no practice** (for a while)! Simply tell pupils that they are *not* to do any practice for a certain time. They will look at you with a combination of puzzlement and suspicion and you'll probably get a call from a parent (*'Tom tells me you've told him not to practise?'*). You could, sensitively, explain the reason. When you feel the old ways have been forgotten and especially if pupils begin to ask you *'When can I start doing some practice?'* you'll know the time has clearly arrived to re-introduce it, but as a very different activity.

The Simultaneous Learning Practice Map is a revolutionary new approach to the way we prescribe what pupils are to do in their practice. It moves a long way away from the itemised list, which is so often completely ignored. The Practice Map is a representation of the lesson and, more interestingly still, it's a representation of what goes on in a pupil's mind. It takes on board the organic nature of learning and it makes practice so much more meaningful, attractive and understandable.

4 The problem with practice

> 'It's the 'idea' of practising that is the problem, but once practising starts, it's okay.'
> YoYo Ma

The ultimate success of our pupils is, to quite an extent, dependent on whether they actually do any practice. We see them, on average, for between twenty and forty minutes a week. Not *that* much learning happens in the lesson. The real learning happens when pupils go home and explore, develop and process the ideas on their own and in their own way, integrating new ideas with those that they already have, through their own experience of the world and using their own vocabulary. The ability to practise positively and productively is therefore absolutely central to a musician's development.

I hope you will feel stimulated to consider the exciting new approach I have outlined in the previous chapters, and in later chapters we will develop these ideas further in all sorts of ways. Pupils should begin to see practice in a new light. But in this chapter I would like to discuss why pupils have, over generations, found practice so troublesome and often such a struggle – it is very important for us to have some idea of these reasons. We will inevitably meet pupils for whom getting down to practice is a major problem; this knowledge will allow us to be sympathetic and helpful.

What are your own memories of practice as a child? Take a few minutes to think back and consider them. How much practice did you do then, and how much do you do now? What are your present expectations of your pupils' practice? Don't forget, *you* have become a professional musician – your enthusiasms, instincts and energy have brought you to where you are now. Each of our pupils will have their own personalities and aspirations, and our expectations therefore need to be adjusted appropriately.

'I never use the word *practice*'

I've known a number of people who think the *word itself* is the problem. When spoken, it's neither a particularly lovely nor ugly sounding word. They prefer to use other words instead – 'playing' for example, or 'research'. But there's nothing wrong with the word – it's all the associations that generate the negativity. Young learners over many generations have been led into practice in ways that were clearly destined to result in boredom, fear, resentfulness and a host of other negative reactions, none of which are likely to promote anything other than a deep dislike and disdain for it. Countless numbers of people hold this destructive and harmful view (many of them are our pupils' parents). And these views are often openly shared:

'I hated practice when I was young.'

'My teacher tried to get me to practise scales but I never did.'

'I used to find practice so boring.'

Many young people seem virtually hard-wired with a built-in aversion concept, and hearing these views expressed by their elders doesn't help a

We need to re-wire our pupils' brains so that when they think of practice, they think positive thoughts. This won't happen overnight – we're going to have to chip away at it. We have to teach a new generation that practice *is* fun. We will be able to do this – it will just take a little dedication and a little resourcefulness.

Let's have a look at some of the problems in more detail.

It isn't turning out as expected

> *I am practising but I don't seem to be making much progress.*

Many pupils think progress is going to be much faster than it actually turns out to be. The kind of progress many would like to make (especially on certain instruments) really can take time. Additionally, if technical progress is high on a teacher's agenda, then it all becomes rather difficult and frustrating. We need to ensure that expectations are always realistic and that work set for practice will provide lots of opportunities for *discernable* achievement and positive feelings of pleasure.

A darker version of this: *'I am practising but it doesn't seem to make any difference'* may suggest pupils in victim mode. We must do our best to turn these negative thoughts around by using the Simultaneous Practice Cycle and setting up more opportunities for positive achievement. Eventually we should be able to bring about more constructive and optimistic thinking.

Time management

> *I'm too busy ...*

What exactly does that mean? We need to help pupils establish a kind of hierarchy of activities, as just *doing something* does not necessarily amount to being busy! Many adults are *too busy*, always engaged in some kind of frenetic activity. But frequently this is a bit of a smoke screen, used as an excuse for avoiding doing something less appealing. Children will often seize on this pretext for not practising – it sounds very grown-up and convincing. Of course, a great many of our pupils are engaged in a lot of interesting and worthy activities during a typical week, so we do need to offer help and guidance in working out how to fit some regular practice into their daily lives. In a sense we are competing for their quality time. But sometimes they may be indulging in less worthwhile activities and we need to feel confident to talk about these.

:ople have the idea that pupils should work towards thirty minutes as
num length of a practice session. But a shorter practice session is
te acceptable (particularly if on a regular basis) – even five minutes is
ian nothing if a pupil really is that busy.

ying priorities

:e is considered by pupils to be low priority, equivalent perhaps to helping
ie house or tidying their bedrooms, then they are understandably going
to struggle to do much. As they become more involved in the Simultaneous
Practice Cycle their whole approach will begin to put practice much higher in
their scheme of things: perhaps even level with social networking or watching
TV! It is worth having some idea of where it does fit, particularly in pupils we
inherit from other teachers.

Fear of failure and criticism

'I can't be expected to play well if I haven't practised.'

This is a very common and powerful reason why so many shy away from
practice. No one likes to fail and few enjoy being criticized. Inappropriate
expectations create the conditions for failure. If practice is set up in a way
that results in poor work (pupils don't really understand what's to be done
or perhaps it's all too difficult) and they know that they will probably receive
disapproval of some sort at the next lesson, the best solution is not to do any.
By not practising pupils will have created (in their own minds) a good reason
for not playing well. *'My teacher may get annoyed that I can't play well, but it
doesn't count because I haven't practised.'*

It's a counter-productive viewpoint resulting from a negative kind of logic, but
it is very understandable. This kind of thinking is often triggered by the over-
demanding, outcome-led teacher who has inappropriate expectations and
tends to set practice in a one-size-fits-all kind of way, irrespective of the needs
and disposition of the pupil. Some over-pressurising parents have a lot to
answer for here, too.

Fear of failure is a serious problem for high-achieving pupils who may have
been continually praised for their talent (or labelled 'talented') and so develop
a serious need to protect that label. If they are given a challenging task that
they can't see how to accomplish, they may lose confidence and their response
will be to avoid it. Many highly promising young musicians have failed to fulfil
their promise owing to too much judgemental praise[10]: too much praise for
ability. It's a salutary lesson – always remember, praise effort as much as you
like; praise ability with caution.

10 See chapter 4
of *The Virtuoso
Teacher* (Faber
Music).

Boredom

If what we expect pupils to do is perceived as boring then it's unlikely to be
done – or at best done without enthusiasm. It is important to remember that
it's not in any way mandatory to learn a musical instrument or to sing – often

our pupils do it by choice. If practice is not perceived as an enjoyable activity (this doesn't in any way preclude hard work!) then, except perhaps for some unusually dedicated individuals, we can't really *expect* it to be done.

If pupils admit to being bored by practice we must be sensitive to their feelings and not simply dismiss them. If they feel they are being listened to and taken seriously then they are more likely to be open to ideas to help them move forward.

Practice does need to be 'fun'. Sometimes when I mention this to teachers they baulk at the word. In dictionary terms, the word fun is the opposite of boring. Fun in this context is not frivolous, but it implies an activity that is by turns purposeful, engaging, stimulating, exciting, worthwhile, meaningful and heartfelt. I think this is the appropriate definition and is certainly my interpretation of the word.

Confusion

A lack of practice may be the result of pupils simply not understanding the prescribed task. If they are confused or anxious in any way there will be no enthusiasm or motivation to find the necessary energy to take the flute out of its case or open the piano lid. If pupils are sent home with ideas only half understood, practice will not be pleasurable or productive. There is no clear route towards achievement. And because of the lack of productive practice, the pupil will come to expect a lack of enthusiasm from the teacher at the next lesson. It's a recipe for failure.

Overwhelmed by the task

'Where do I start?'

Another reason for lack of practice occurs when pupils feel there is just too much to do. If it's a question to which they can find no ready solution, then *'Nowhere'* is likely to be the answer. Being overwhelmed by the task is actually quite a dangerous place to be. Pupils may draw the conclusion that they're overwhelmed because they lack musical ability. This will result in a loss of self-esteem, which will soon cause a further loss of motivation, which will mean less practice, losing interest, and eventually giving up. That is not the outcome we would desire. Precisely what we give pupils to practise is very important, and we'll discuss this in Chapter 6.

Occasionally pupils may not practise because they are underwhelmed by the expectation. *'It's all too easy – I don't really need to do any practice.'*

Laziness

Very few people are inherently lazy. Laziness is specifically connected to particular tasks and activities. Few children behave lazily when it comes to doing something they really want to do. If pupils are not practising through what looks like laziness we must dig deeper. Being 'lazy' is almost always the result of some other factor (or factors). Some of the reasons above may give the impression that the pupil is lazy, but in fact the laziness may be brought about by:

- a lack of understanding
- too little self-belief that the work could be achieved
- the feeling that the teacher set inappropriate work
- too much or too little to do
- work that the pupil distinctly did not want to be given that week.

There are many possibilities. Try to explore sensitively to find out where the problem lies and gently move forward.

Learned Helplessness

'I can't do it, so I won't do it.'

If a teacher continually sets work that is too demanding, or has a list of practice requirements that can never be fully met, causing the pupil to fall short on a regular basis, that pupil may well develop the attributes of 'Learned Helplessness'. Such pupils will display a lack of energy and lose any sense of motivation. Eventually they will probably use Learned Helplessness as a reason for their failure and ultimately for giving up.

Teach pupils to take a more positive and less personal approach to things they 'can't do'. Rather than *'I can't play that bit'*, teach them to think objectively: *'Those two notes aren't even, that's why it's not sounding good.'*

Withholding

'I can do it – but I won't do it.'

This desire to manipulate usually comes from a deep insecurity, a fear of failure and a fear of being judged. If someone feels 'out of self-control' or insecure they will often attempt to control others, and those pupils who try to control their teachers (mostly by non-cooperation) are difficult to manage. First of all we must remain untainted by their negativity, we must never get frustrated, irritated or annoyed. We must accept their viewpoint unconditionally, slowly build up their confidence, and play a waiting game. Draw them into the Simultaneous Practice Cycle and, at first anyway, accept the very minimum of practice. With patience, most pupils will probably begin to develop the security to allow them to move out of their unhappy condition.

It's too solitary an activity

Pupils who have low self-esteem, who are perhaps not comfortable with who they are, will probably find it difficult to settle down to practise. Practice is generally a solitary occupation and we have to feel comfortable with being on our own. If you feel a pupil may not be practising for this reason, a very gentle nudge towards just a few minutes a day will be a start. Only gradually increase your expectation for longer practice sessions and ensure that all the work set will result in a very positive sense of achievement. Focus on pieces that your pupil will learn easily and instantly enjoy.

How do we react to pupils who haven't practised?

As we become more sensitive to the reasons pupils might not be practising we will be able to react and talk to them appropriately and sympathetically. If pupils occasionally don't practise our best strategy is simply to move on. Don't dwell on it or even ask for excuses, which is normally just a waste of time (though we wouldn't want to miss the occasional gem!). We should never get annoyed, though there are times when we might display a little irritation – if a pupil has a major audition the next week and no practice seems to be taking place, it wouldn't be out of order! A very occasional 'sharp word' can be a powerful and effective tool for getting results, and reminds the pupil that you really do care – so maybe the activity *is* worth caring about!

Don't provoke feelings of guilt: *'You're letting me/your parents down'*. Guilt usually leads to resentfulness and anger and ultimately revenge (which will take the form of more lack of practice or just giving up). We might suggest to pupils that they are letting themselves down (if you are trying to develop more self-responsibility) but this is a risky strategy and should be used cautiously.

In general, let's be prepared to take responsibility for our pupils' lack of practice – if they're not practising it's our fault! We need to work harder to make their practice more desirable.

'My pupils never practise!' is *not* the battle cry of the pro-active, imaginative teacher!

As we take more care in prescribing appropriate practice activities for our pupils and as more teachers begin to adopt the Simultaneous Practice Cycle, fewer pupils will struggle with the concept. But this will take time. In the interim, let's consider each pupil and their relationship with practice with care, sensitivity and open eyes. Young people today are so often already under a lot of stress; let's do our best not to add to it, but instead to see that they view practice as an important and fulfilling part of their lives. Indeed, playing music can often be a way to escape from stress. And it's something that, occasionally, will provide peer-group respect as well as self-respect and the approval of adults.

5 'Do I *have* to practise?'

Of course you do ...

And the reason why is pretty obvious, isn't it? We practise to *improve* and to *progress*. If practice is done reasonably efficiently then these two worthy outcomes should always materialize, whether in the short, medium or long term. But perhaps we could be a little more perceptive and broaden our thinking here. If practice is just to improve and to progress then we set the stage for potential disappointment, possible frustration and general stress. There are other beneficial and valuable 'reasons' to practise, and we're going to consider them in this chapter. We will see how they impact on improving and progressing and how they will help relieve the stress that is so often associated with practice.

If we adopt the Simultaneous Practice Cycle, then pupils should soon begin to assimilate intuitively the central reason for practising: it's simply part of the organic, ongoing process, resulting in playing or singing to whatever standard pupils aspire. This awareness should be allowed to develop naturally and unconsciously – we may never actually talk about it with our pupils.

Let's look at some other reasons why we practise.

'Because I love it'

Why do beginners practise? Certainly to improve. But beginners simply enjoy *doing* their music: they practise because they love it. If they are being taught imaginatively, they will practise to **explore** and to **experiment**. Practice is perceived entirely as a positive and exhilarating adventure. Beginners haven't experienced much failure. They are lost in a frenzy of highly motivated and enthusiastic learning.

Somehow we must do our best to maintain this relish for practice. Ultimately, why do any of us practise? I hope it's to enjoy the profound pleasures of music-making – it makes us feel good. It also satisfies our basic instincts of enquiry and curiosity. The twin concepts of exploration and experimentation must therefore always play their part. As you introduce new ingredients, whether connected with technique, musical expression, control of tone-colour or whatever else, always try to do so with imagination and in a spirit of discovering something new for the first time. Whatever level a pupil may be, show them how to *explore* and *experiment* with that new ingredient. If we set up practice so that pupils rarely fail, the chances of sustaining the beginners' sense of pleasure is much more likely. That doesn't mean avoiding challenges; as long as pupils believe they will eventually succeed, these can still be part of practice. It's simply ensuring pupils are always in control of their practice. If we manage that, then we are well on the way to maintaining that relish.

Endorphins

Sometimes – not always – positive and concentrated practice can make us feel physically good. Like exercising, eating spicy foods and laughing, practising can release endorphins: chemicals that enter our bloodstream and literally cheer us up. Make sure that pupils always have something new, however small, that they will be able to master: a particular technique, shaping a simple phrase beautifully, creating an entrancing tone colour. All can create very powerful responses and will leave pupils (and us) feeling really exhilarated.

Let me think ...

Practising gives us the opportunity to focus our thinking, at many levels. As we teach pupils to use the Simultaneous Learning Practice Map they will need our help to learn about the important ability to make informed choices.

> *Should I make a connection to aural or theory next?*
> *Which would be the more helpful?*

There are literally endless aspects of music that pupils need to think about:

> *What would be the best dynamic at which to begin this piece?*
> *What speed should I play this? Which note represents the peak of this phrase? How shall I approach and exit from this trill? Where shall I use the pedal? Is that interval really in tune?*

We need to teach pupils to ask themselves these questions.

In fact we need to teach pupils to think *actively*. If we don't, they probably won't. A lot of practice is done with the brain disengaged. It goes without saying how much more satisfying it becomes when pupils learn to think about what they are doing: the difference this will make to the value of practice will be huge. As soon as we are thinking about the next activity, and how we are connecting with that activity, it becomes so much more focused and purposeful.

In fact much of our dialogue with pupils should be in the form of questions. Remember, telling is not teaching. *'Which note do you think we should make the crest of this phrase?'* is so much more powerful than simply informing a pupil to *'Make this note the peak of this phrase'*.

Enrichment

> *'Although I quite enjoyed practising, when I reached the age of eleven and joined a band the penny dropped – music was a team game and many individuals added up to something wonderful! From that point there was no need for my parents to make me practise.'*
> John

As a result of practice (with its attendant outcomes of improvement and progress) pupils can find themselves taking part in ensembles, choirs, orchestras and bands, playing duets and accompanying their friends. All these experiences add value to their lives: they have become truly enriched through their practice. Their enjoyment of music as listeners is also enhanced. Hearing music, whether live or recorded, becomes a deeper experience through the pupils' own musical understanding and involvement.

Additionally, practice can stimulate a number of deeper benefits that affect the very way we are.

Self-awareness

Because we are teaching pupils to think more deeply during their practice, it is only a small leap forward to encourage them to think about their own behaviour, responses and reactions. As they do so they will also start to get much more out of practice on a deeper level.

Once pupils begin to develop self-awareness, the following kinds of thoughts should seep into their consciousness:

✓ I'm practising …
✓ I'm enjoying it …
✓ I can see how it works.
✓ This is useful … This is fun.
✓ I can see how this will affect my potential progress.
✓ I am aware of my actual progress.
✓ That didn't work so I'll try something different next time.
✓ I'm looking forward to the lesson and the reaction of my teacher to what I've done.

In addition, they will become more able to deal with a variety of situations. They will learn how to control possible frustrations, difficulties and perhaps passing disappointments in a level-headed and positive manner. They are learning from their experiences.

To be constructively self-critical

The ability to be *constructively* self-critical is extremely important. If something doesn't work it's all too easy to play the victim – *I can't do this. I'm no good.* This is so often followed by a dive into negativity and a loss of direction. Instead let's teach pupils to be more objective and try to find their own solutions. Acknowledge that something went wrong and then look for another way. *'That didn't work so I wonder what I can try instead?'*

Self-esteem

Pupils need to develop self-esteem, which simply means that they are comfortable with who they are. This in turn will give them the confidence to cultivate opinions and make informed decisions. Self-esteem helps pupils to achieve their potential. It will help them to work through problems positively. It's easy to assist the development of self-esteem: just being very positive in our response to their practice will do the trick. At the 'connection' point of the Simultaneous Practice Cycle, the beginning of the lesson, we show real interest in what they've thought about and done; we take their ideas and use them to move the lesson forward. Genuine respect for our pupils will help them to develop their own self-respect. It's as simple as that.

Fuelling the imagination

Practice will certainly help pupils to develop their imaginations, provided we direct them in the right way. Young children have very active imaginations and when teaching beginners we should feed into that regularly. Encourage them to make up vivid stories to fit the music (the more outrageous, zany, funny, annoying or sombre the better). Improvise from virtually any interesting starting point, be it the title, a musical ingredient or phrase from their piece, or a shape, smell, colour or taste. Even when pupils get older and more self-conscious let's try to find ways of encouraging them to involve their imagination. The ways we suggest just have to be a little more sophisticated. I've never known a pupil of any age who didn't respond to a striking or funny image or metaphor, and inspiring them to reflect on their music in this way when practising will add another level of interest.

Getting organised

As we gradually train our pupils to engage naturally and regularly with practice we can also begin to encourage them to become more organised. Many writers on practice, for example, have expressed views on the best times of day for practising (some say before or after breakfast, some say in the evening, some say at the same time each day and so on). In fact it's different for each pupil. For some, practising virtually the moment after they've woken up *is* the ideal time; others may not be able to string a sentence together, let alone the notes of a C sharp minor arpeggio! Many young people really are busy, so the same time every day may be impractical. So it's a useful point of discussion. Hand in hand with organisational skill comes self-responsibility, which we should help pupils develop without ever invoking guilt. Certainly, in the case of most young learners, the responsibility for actually doing any practice is their own. If pupils really don't want to practise, they won't.

Boosting the individual

As pupils develop their musical abilities we can help them to begin to cultivate a personal and individual approach. We take their ideas seriously: their stories behind pieces they are learning, their thoughts on shaping a phrase, a piece they desperately want to learn. We support their opinions and ideas. We respect their values. We may wish to discuss and perhaps moderate them, but taking pupils seriously is very important. I've heard many a horror story about teachers, often at advanced levels, who put down their pupils' ideas in favour of their own – that's a very ego-led and destructive way to behave.

There are probably even more benefits and personal qualities that are positively influenced through practice. Musical and technical improvement and progress are undoubtedly at the very centre of our reasons for practising. But let's not limit our thinking. We must realise the broader potential for self-development that practice can generate. One of the most important advantages is that these broader reasons for practising can put improvement and progress into a more realistic and manageable perspective.

6 What we actually *do* during that time we call practice

> *'Practice is the search for ever greater joy in movement and expression.'*
> Yehudi Menuhin

Let me begin by asking you a surprisingly tricky question. Can you, in a short sentence, express what pupils should do when they practise? You don't have to grapple with it, of course, but I'd really like you to try before reading on. Here it is again:

What should pupils do when they practise?

Here are a number of responses from teachers:

'Think about what I taught them and then do their best to bring those ideas to life.'

'Have fun playing their instrument.'

'Go over what we did in the lesson, work at what they can't do and correct their mistakes.'

'A lot of thinking.'

Some responses from parents:

'Work for about half an hour a day and concentrate hard.'

'Practise a lot with a metronome and remember to do all the markings.'

'Whatever they want to play.'

'Work on the things they were taught in the lesson and try to perfect them.'

'Anything musical.'

And some responses from pupils:

'Go over the stuff from the lesson.'

'Try to get my scales right.'

'It's just something I have to do – I don't think about it really.'

'Repeat exercises until I can do them correctly.'

'Go over the things I can't do.'

'Play the bits I get stuck on.'

'Play through my favourite pieces.'

'Play my pieces until I get them fluent.'

'Get my instrument out and play it for twenty minutes.'

'I just grab my clarinet and start playing.'

...o how do pupils *actually* spend their time during their practice sessions? ...lot many work with the focus and discipline that we may desire (despite our ...best efforts).

- A considerable number will simply go through the motions with their brains pretty much disengaged. They will play their pieces through a few times, maybe stopping to correct a mistake (but more likely not), and then perhaps play a scale or two (the ones they know).
- Some will do things too quickly and thoughtlessly, often playing un-rhythmically, with little or no musical expression, adding more (unnoticed and uncorrected) mistakes to those they already make.
- Some will dutifully do exactly what they are told but without much thinking or imagination, causing restricted and often rather rigid musical learning.
- Some will spend the time thinking about other things or worrying about why they can't do what they've been asked.
- Some will just sit (or stand) doing very little.
- Some will go through the motions while watching the television or thinking about anything other than what they're actually doing.

None of the above is of much use really. It's mostly just wasting time. But before we look into what pupils should do in that time called *practice*, let's look at **four long-held practice beliefs** that need putting into perspective.

1 Have a specific 'to do' list

We've already discussed the kinds of itemised linear lists that fill up so many pupils' notebooks. Such lists are often likely to cause anxiety (*'I haven't managed to get through what my teacher wanted!'*) and they are often not understood – or simply ignored.

The Practice Map offers a very different approach.

2 Practising is all about improving technique and working at pieces, carefully and in detail

No one would argue with this. By assimilating technical control we free the mind to concentrate on the musical and communicative aspects of the piece. While that may come easily and make perfect sense for some pupils, it won't for others. Our intentions must be to encourage *more* pupils to practise and enjoy the wonderful benefits of being musical.

So whilst improving technique and working at pieces remain central, we need to search for other areas to broaden the scope of practice and thus help us to retain more pupils.

3 Practice should include lots of repetition

Practice will inevitably include repetition – physical movements (technique), rhythms, learning ways to control sounds and more. This kind of practice is very important: if we repeat an action a sufficient number of times we literally hard-wire our brains (that's why practised mistakes are so difficult to unpack). But let's take the view that including lots of repetitive work during practice may lead to boredom, a draining of energy and general disenchantment unless introduced and developed very much on a 'need to do' basis *in collaboration with the pupil*. If the pupil can see its relevance and wants to do some, then by all means, with appropriate care, include some repetitive work.

Mindful repetitive practice becomes increasingly necessary of course for those moving forwards into a more advanced world of playing, and it will become increasingly acceptable as pupils become more mature and understand exactly what they are doing and why they are doing it. But do handle it with care – it can so easily put pupils off. Mind*less* repetition should always be discouraged – it just wastes time.

Allow the idea of mindful repetitive work to develop gradually through experimentation. In the section *Create feasible and fun targets: 'personal bests' and mini-outcomes* (on page 47) you'll find a fun way into repetitive practice.

4 Mistakes should always be corrected promptly

For many teachers a mistake that isn't corrected immediately is a serious offence. Which is fine – naturally we don't want our pupils to *learn* mistakes. But it is unlikely that many pupils will be able to live up to this request. The trouble is that it's difficult to fix a mistake if you don't know you've made one. And that's what so often happens: most pupils don't understand sufficiently well to play without mistakes, or indeed to know that they've made any.

And if we are stuck in a teaching world that is very much centred on *mistake correction*, pupils will simply continue to make mistakes – which of course they do.

So our intention must be to get ourselves into the positive, pro-active Simultaneous Learning world where mistakes rarely occur and teaching is not a catalogue of mistake correction. If we are predominantly in the Simultaneous Learning world and our pupils are learning in this positive way, then mistakes should be few and far between. If pupils do make them, they know, because they understand what they are doing.

Ideally, when playing longer phrases, we should teach our pupils not to stop if they make a mistake. Instead, they should make a mental note of it and correct it later, especially when there is a bit of a *flow* going on. Focusing on mistakes breaks the flow. It stops pupils being creative. Let's encourage pupils to enjoy the sensation of playing without stopping, to enjoy the musical experience.

Come back to that mistake later and work at it positively and creatively. Teach pupils to treat mistakes as features of interest. Why was it made and how can it be corrected next time? There's absolutely nothing wrong with making mistakes if pupils understand why they made them and respond constructively.

> Do think about and perhaps review your approach to these last four points. Coming at them from a slightly different angle will help to take a lot of the stress out of practice.

What pupils *should* do

If we begin to put the Simultaneous Practice Cycle into effect we should begin to see a much more positive and productive use of time developing. I'd like to suggest a number of activities which will give practice sessions more variety and make them feel more enticing. There are in fact seven options on the menu that I call the *Seven Elements*. Sometimes a number of them will play their part, at other times, just a few; occasionally a whole session might just be made up of one of these elements. Let's see what they are.

The Seven Elements

1 *Physical warm-ups*

I begin every lesson with some physical warm-ups and relaxation exercises designed to loosen tensions (as much as is possible in a few minutes), develop a good posture, prepare muscles that are going to be exercised, and put the pupil in the best mental state for an effective lesson.

I have a regular routine which I hope all my pupils will learn over time and then repeat at the start of a practice session. All teachers should have their own set of warm-ups which need to be understood and imitated in practice. Such exercises are necessary for all pupils and especially for your more dedicated students who may practise for longer periods of time. Uncomfortable, even painful tensions (in the neck or upper back, for example) could curtail or spoil good practice or do more lasting damage, and must be avoided at all costs.

> ### Brain states
>
> A word about what is known as 'brain states' or brain activity. Much research into this fascinating area has been taking place over recent years. Presently, scientists have identified seven brain states, from *Delta* (deep sleep) through to *Super High Beta* (a state of extremely high alertness). We need only concern ourselves with two: *Beta*, our normal waking state, and *Alpha* – a very pleasant state of relaxation and reduced stress, where heightened creativity and learning can flourish. Practice and lessons will be much more productive and effective if pupils (and indeed teachers!) connect, to some degree, with *Alpha* state. There's nothing mysterious, otherworldly or 'spiritual' about this and *it doesn't mean any reduction of mental or physical energy*. All we need to do is some gentle and slow deep breathing exercises and we instantly increase our Alpha activity.[11] It really is as simple as that.
>
> This will also be useful for adult learners (especially adult beginners) who often carry around a lot of stress and pressures from their daily lives.

11 For example, breathe in for four beats, hold your breath for four beats and breathe out for four beats at ♩ = 60. Repeat two or three times.

2 *Thinking*

Is practice without thinking really practice? Probably not. We need to teach our pupils that practice begins with *the brain turned on*. The first thought should generally be: *'What did we do in the lesson?'* Then, armed with a Practice Map, the voyage of discovery begins, with imagination (we hope) also at the ready.

But before we move on, let's look at that thought in a bit more detail, because it really is rather fascinating. *'What* did *we do in the lesson?'*

Supposing you gave exactly the same lesson to two or more pupils, what each remembers would be surprisingly different. What we remember about any experience is very personal. It will be influenced by what we already know, what we deeply understand, what catches our imaginations, what we enjoy or amuses us and what surprises or perhaps even shocks us. We remember what we particularly notice, what particularly interests us, and things that make a logical and strong connection to what we already understand. That is why it is so important that the Practice Map is filled out *in collaboration* with pupils. They are much more likely to recall ideas and activities that they themselves represented on the map. So the answer to *'What did we do in the lesson?'* becomes much more vivid and clear.

There are many other important thoughts we can begin to teach our pupils to have. One set is concerned with planning, monitoring and evaluating the session; another set is to do with *thinking about* ... the title, the ingredients, the character, the composer, aspects of theory and so on.

Planning is important: knowing where we are going makes the journey so much more productive. But our pupils won't have to do that much planning because it will have all been set up in the lesson. Working around the map will supply all the ingredients and activities that will go to make up an engaging and enjoyable, productive and well-directed practice session. In this way, we are setting up 'purposeful' or 'deliberate' practice (more of which in Chapter 10). The more advanced pupil may need to plan their sessions more systematically, and if an exam or audition is looming then of course all the appropriate work needs to be factored in. But DO help – most pupils will not work hard unless you do! One helpful teacher I know prepares (on paper) a very comprehensive grid where pupils tick off each element as they complete it. Another uses a similar idea, but the pupil logs in to the teacher's webpage and indicates progress there. What works best for you and your pupils?

As far as monitoring and evaluating work goes, the beginner may like to ask themselves:

> *'What should I do next?'*

and then an important follow-up question:

> *'Did that go well?'*

For the developing pupil:

> *'What do I need to think carefully about?'*
> *'What connections can I usefully make?'*
> *'I'll try this connection because I think it will help.'*

Then adding:

> 'Did I do it well? Could I have done it differently or more effectively?'

The more advanced pupil may like to follow this process:

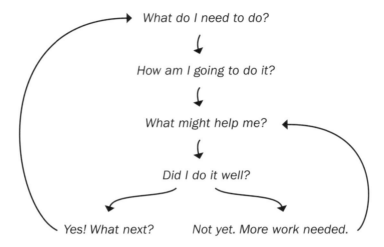

What do I need to do?

How am I going to do it?

What might help me?

Did I do it well?

Yes! What next?   Not yet. More work needed.

Perhaps adding:

'How will what I know already help with this? Or do I need to learn anything new to understand this?'

Thinking carefully (sometimes deeply) about what we do will help to bring out real progress at any level. Pupils will *know* that they can do things. They won't have to keep their fingers crossed that things will work in the next lesson. It will take a lot of anxiety out of the process.

12 I use the word flow here to mean effortless engagement. The Hungarian psychologist Mihaly Csikszentmihali has written fascinatingly about this.

As pupils improve at this, whether at beginner, intermediate or advanced levels of practice, the necessity for interrupting their efforts with these thoughts diminishes. As a sense of *flow*[12] increases, the necessity for deliberate monitoring becomes less and less. It will happen naturally as pupils begin to lose themselves in a practice session in which they are fully engaged and really enjoying.

Also encourage pupils to *think about* particular elements: the title and character of their pieces through improvisation and exploration of the ingredients, for example. Encourage them to find out something about the composer perhaps, or some theory element (which, for some, can be fascinating). *'This piece has a flat in the key-signature – see if you can find out how the flat sign developed.' 'We're going to learn an arpeggio this week, where does that word actually come from?'*

3 Musical warm-ups

Musical warm-ups may be done in association with the Practice Map or may be a stand-alone activity, designed to turn on the imagination and start the musical mind flowing. If you are familiar with the **Four Ps**[13] they will help shape a very comprehensive set of musical warm-ups guaranteed to get these all-important elements of musical development underway:

13 See *Teaching Beginners* (Faber Music) page 8.

Posture: This has already been taken care of (see *Physical warm-ups* above).

Pulse: Pupils clap a steady pulse in the time and character of their piece. Perhaps they include some of the rhythms under consideration too.

Phonology (control of sound): Pupils play/sing a note and listen to the sound, then play/sing it in different ways and at varying dynamic levels, connected to the varying characteristics of their piece/song where possible.

Personality (of the music): Pupils create short improvisations to portray different characters relevant to the piece/song they are learning.

I use this format for all pupils from beginner to diploma level! It just takes a little imagination to adapt it for any pupil. Do insist (as you would in a lesson) that pupils immerse themselves as deeply and with as much concentration as possible in these warm-ups. When they play a note, for example, they *really* listen to it – to its quality, to how it begins and ends and whether it changes, and to its tuning. This kind of attention really does make a difference.

Just to remain with the Four Ps for a moment longer: we know that if *all* lessons are driven by the Four Ps then those lessons *will* be effective – from the very first lesson onwards. The same goes for practice. If we set practice up so that all pupils touch upon each of these pillars of learning, we can be assured that the session will be comprehensive and successful. For pupils at *any* level and whatever their particular aspirations may be, the Four Ps are a real constant.

4 Engaging with music through the instrument or voice

Many see this as the heart of practice. The *pre-eminent* element of the seven. It will include working on pieces and appropriate technical work connected to those pieces; experimenting and exploring; connecting ingredients through improvising or making up exercises. All these activities are connected by our careful Practice Map preparation. Using Simultaneous Learning and simply continuing in the same way during practice will allow all this to happen very effectively.

Strategies used to practise pieces, exercises, studies and scale patterns are the subjects most fully covered by the many books available on practice. They offer much detailed description of how, for example, to practise specific technical matters, how to break pieces down into small manageable units each of which will need particular care and attention. These are worthy strategies that should be incorporated as pupils develop their musical and technical skills and we shall have a look at some of them in a moment. But we want a world where more than just a few exceptional pupils 'make it'. We want to see more of our pupils stick with music and take it forward, in their own way, so that their lives are ultimately significantly enriched. This requires a more flexible and broad-minded approach that certainly sees such strategies as important, but perhaps more as first among equals, rather than the heart itself.

Practice techniques

The main theme of this book is to offer ways to make practice an appealing *psychological* place to be. Most teachers are aware of established and well-founded classic practice techniques (like varying the rhythms, practising slowly or simplifying passages). But here I would like to consider a number of these important practice technique principles in the context of Simultaneous Learning.

Breaking a piece down into manageable chunks

'When my parents lived in New York they owned one of the finest Steinway pianos in the city. A world-famous pianist (Emil Gilels) heard about it and asked to use it for a practice session. My parents were delighted, and sat in the adjoining room with coffee and snacks, expecting to have this outstanding musician give them a recital, even though he was 'just practising'. He duly arrived, sat at the piano, and for well over an hour played three notes, over and over, and in different ways, until he was satisfied. And then he left.'
Uwe

As part of learning a piece, this is perhaps the most classic of all practice techniques, but in fact it's also what we do in Simultaneous Learning: continually breaking down activities into a series of achievable steps. If we teach in the Simultaneous Learning manner, this kind of practice will simply happen automatically. As long as we ensure pupils really understand the ingredients and exactly what they are to practise – whether it's simply starting a note, a finger movement, a shift, controlling a staccato note, tuning an interval or something more involved like shaping a short phrase or working at a longer passage. We spend time discussing how it can be practised by breaking it down into small and manageable constituent parts. For *every* 'difficult' manoeuvre there is always an easy starting point. 'Difficult' is just an opinion, a temporary state or point of view. Suppose a pupil has a tricky three-note figure that just won't sound even: break it down into two lots of two notes and work at them individually, eventually putting them together when the individual technical movements are mastered. The pupil might work at this small fragment (on and off) as part of a single session or may return to it, if necessary, in further sessions. No problem is insoluble.

Slow practice

Another old favourite, and without doubt a very useful strategy. But I would like to suggest taking the concept slightly further and thinking of it as literally practising in *slow-motion*. Practising slowly really means that each pulse is elongated – there is more time before we arrive at the next beat. But having given ourselves that time, we don't always make best use of it.

Slow-motion practice proposes two extensions of the idea: one is that we have more time to *think* about what is going on as we are doing it. *'I'm about to play C sharp ...' 'I'm about to move my third finger ...' 'I'm making a crescendo through this note towards the one after the next ...' 'I'm intensifying the tonal colour of this note ...'* and so on. Secondly we can actually *do* each thing *in slow-motion*. Move fingers or breathe more slowly, move the bow slower, draw out the crescendo. It actually gives us time for very focused and detailed thinking about the action as well as controlling each physical movement with considerable detail as we make it. This is developing our *kinaesthetic awareness* to a high level.

Internalizing

Hearing music in our head is a very useful and powerful ability and if we teach the Simultaneous Learning way all our pupils will, from lesson one, begin to develop the technique. In practice, imagining a note, a phrase or passage or even a whole piece internally – with all the appropriate expression and shape – is invaluable prior to playing it.

Mental practice of technique (visualisation)

Technique can also be practised mentally and this is a useful connection in a Simultaneous Learning activity sequence. *Think* the physical movement very precisely either before making it, or after making it and before repeating it (which is a very strong embedding sequence). Thinking through an awkward movement or the accurate fingering of a scale away from the instrument (on a journey or when trying to get to sleep, for example) can be very effective in developing the skill. Feel the movements in your fingers, bowing arm or tongue. They say that athletes can literally learn to run faster or jump higher just through mind imaging.

5 Listening to music

'Listening' is one of the bubbles on the Practice Map. We should **always** fill it in and encourage pupils to listen to music and watch performers on a regular basis. Looking for pieces they are learning (which will almost certainly be on the Internet) either to listen to or (even better) to see being performed by a world-class player is highly valuable. To watch others perform is inspiring: trying to copy is a natural instinct and very important in the learning process. It's the way many sports people develop their skills.

Be specific when making your listening suggestion. Pupils will be much more likely to listen when they have a clear objective in mind. Perhaps it is an ingredient that is central to that week's practice: listen to the performer's crisp staccato or range of dynamics in a particular section. Or listen to (and watch) an aspect of technical control – notice how he uses his bow, look carefully at her use of arm weight, look at how far he moves his fingers from the instrument. Perhaps it is some particular aspect of musicianship or interpretation, or just to watch a star player performing. As with all other aspects of practice, ask pupils to describe what they heard, and try to make the next 'Listening' activity connect in some interesting way.

Listening also includes listening to themselves. With all the many recording devices available, do suggest frequent use! Recording just a long note, a phrase or a complete performance of a piece will all be very useful. Teach pupils how to listen objectively and then react positively to what they hear. The long note might have been a little uneven in the middle; the phrase didn't have the shape the pupil thought they were giving it; or perhaps the performance needed a little more rhythmic energy.

Simply listening may occasionally constitute a complete practice session for one day every so often, or even on a regular basis. It's a very worthy activity. I've known young musicians who have been suddenly (and absolutely) captivated and transformed through seeing or hearing a particular performer or performance.

6 Projects

In addition to the work set out on the Practice Map, many children will enjoy putting a project together. And you may be surprised: with the right subject, pupils I never thought would have signed themselves up for this kind of activity have been inspired! Projects may be written down in a scrapbook or on a computer. There are, of course, many different opportunities for research, for example the internet, libraries and visits to appropriate establishments, and there is quite a bit of fun available for those who wish to broaden their awareness. For younger pupils, simply drawing a picture to represent their piece will lead to commitment and interest.

Subjects for consideration might include composers: one pupil of mine really relished finding out about composers, discovered some are actually alive and even got in touch when it was possible. The composers in question were usually very kind and generous in their responses. Instruments lend themselves to fascinating study and again, if your pupil really gets involved, there are instrument museums to be visited. Then there are titles. Have you ever taught a minuet? I suspect most will answer 'yes'! Could you demonstrate the dance movements to your pupils? Could you even describe the dance? I suspect most will be answering 'no' this time. There are many delightful clips of minuets on the Internet, some danced in authentic costume, as well as tutorials showing you exactly how to create the correct steps. Teaching a minuet should never be the same again …

Individual projects may last a few weeks or pupils may prefer *mini projects* that are very focussed and completed in just one week.

7 Creating a personal dossier

Even though it's been many years since children have gone in for stamp collecting, there is something quite addictive about the principle of accumulation. So I'm going to suggest that the modern equivalent is to build a personal dossier, a record of achievement that will be both a permanent reminder of a pupil's musical experiences and a useful document to be shown to a new teacher or to granny. It could be created in book form or it could be set up as an e-document where there is the added advantage of being able to append audio or video files of performances, improvisations and anything else relevant. Here are the elements it could include:

- Lists of pieces/songs learnt with comments.
- Lists (plus audio and/or video files) of performances.
- Selected improvisations (again with audio/video files).

- Progress with the Four Ps.
- Favourite pieces other players have performed.
- Pieces heard (on recordings or played by friends) that have inspired, and why.
- Projects undertaken (on the history or workings of the instrument or on composers, for example).
- Compositions: written or played/recorded.
- Concerts given/attended.
- Pictures collected of themselves playing (or famous players) and the instrument, etc.
- Teachers' contributions.

You'll be surprised, occasionally amazed, at how some pupils really do enjoy this and will want to add to it on a regular basis. Which is how it becomes part of the practice suite of activities: updating the dossier. Indeed, the principle is really just an extension of what many young people do already today as part of their social networking.

There are two additional advantages to the personal dossier. Looking after it and keeping it up to date also provides pupils with a means to self-reflect and self-assess; they are able to view and take ownership of their development. The personal dossier also provides parents with a clear record of their child's musical growth.

Practice should not be an exclusive place, inhabited only by highly self-motivated pupils who seem to have a natural ability to work hard, with focus and discipline. It should be a friendly place where all our pupils can spend some pleasant, enjoyable and stress-free time. By broadening our view of what constitutes effective and acceptable practice, many more pupils could be brought on board, to the general delight of all concerned. We are teaching them to practise music rather than just practise the instrument.

7 Making practice a snug and comfortable place to be

There are a number of additional factors that we can consider and develop to make practice still more desirable for our pupils. I'm not talking here about the physical environment. We can deal with that in very few words, though it is important: if the space is light, at a pleasant temperature and free from too much interruption (with plenty of fresh drinking water available) then we have all we need!

Here we're going to discuss further strategies that will help pupils to perceive practice as a positive and pleasant activity that they really begin to look forward to. Some are practical, some are more psychological, but they all contribute to the development of pupils' overall attitude towards, and perception of, practice.

Everything must be completely crystal clear

When talking about practice it is important to explain with absolute clarity what is to be done, in order to avoid any misunderstanding. It is so easy to fill a pupil with anxiety (often inadvertently) by telling them they should do something which they don't really understand. If we adopt the Practice Map then problems shouldn't arise. We are always working within a pupil's zone of confidence. But just asking a pupil to practise 'this piece' or 'that scale' is almost certainly going to create anxiety, confusion and stress unless it is done with considerable care. *'Do you understand this arpeggio? How much of it would you like to practise?'* If the answer is *'Just the first two notes'* then that's fine. Let's have a week just practising the first two notes, or more weeks if necessary. And then when that pupil feels really comfortable with the first two notes, the time has come to introduce the third. Never be impatient.

Take care when sending pupils home to learn things that haven't been covered in the lesson (except in the case of more advanced pupils or those who you feel really have grasped concepts and are happy and able to apply them to new material). It's all too easy to say *'We haven't had time to do this scale ... this section ... have a go at it at home'*. That's okay if you're certain the pupil is at ease with it. But if there is any uncertainty, then we are creating a potential problem which may take a lot of time in the future to put right.

Less is more

We often set too much (we often teach too much!). The danger here is two-fold. Firstly, if we constantly set more than pupils are capable of doing, they *learn not to take our practice list seriously. 'I only ever do about half of what my teacher sets'* is not a healthy situation. Look forward to the day when a pupil comes to you and says, *'You didn't give me enough to practise last week!'* At this point we can encourage pupils to think about how they might like to develop their practice themselves. For pupils who are living in the world of the Practice

Map this should be no problem. They will know how to de'
finding more to do will be easy! Secondly, setting pupils m
leaves them with ever-deepening feelings of guilt. I have sp
who, in retrospect, reluctantly gave up their music as the g
to unhappy levels.

Awakening the pupil's desire to practise

'I rarely practised what was given to me by my teacher, but spent hours happily trawling through the piano stool which was full of loads of fascinating sheet music.'
Rowan

In general (and in reality), most pupils will only practise what they want to practise. They'll practise best what they really understand and what they consider is appropriate and relevant. It's worth us keeping this in the back of our minds when agreeing the week's activities. That doesn't mean they won't practise what we want them to. It just means we have to present the work in a reasoned and palatable fashion. *'If you work through these connections and spend some quality time on this technical point, things will move swiftly forward and soon you'll be able to play this piece with real conviction.'* That's aspirational talk and, if they truly believe this to be the case (based on former experience, perhaps), few will be able to resist it. They will go home with a strong desire to practise.

It's also important to feed pupils with lots of ambition. Play to them and demonstrate regularly (avoid showing off though) so they always have a clear model of what they can achieve. Set up concerts so that they can hear and see their peers playing. Perhaps they might want to play the same piece or realise that some technique is actually within their reach. Place learning firmly within their comfort zones, for example by suggesting regular and appropriate music to listen to and watch on internet sites. These are all strong motivational strategies. Pupils have often brought me pieces they want to learn, usually pieces friends are playing. Motivational levels are very high and a lot of learning takes place. See how often you can create the situation where a pupil actually comes in and asks you *'Can you teach me this ...?'*

Create feasible and fun targets: 'personal bests' and mini-outcomes

For the many pupils who love computer games of one sort or another (or any kind of healthy competitive activity), let's make use of one particularly relevant feature: the *personal best* factor. Many young people love to beat their personal best and to compare theirs with those of their friends. So let's take advantage of this each week by providing a gentle challenge. It will usually find its way into the Technique or unlabelled bubble of the Practice Map. This may take a bit of imagination and thought on our part but it can be hugely motivating. It's usually going to begin with a *'how many ...'* or *'how long ...'* type direction.

Here are a few:

- How many times can you play a G major scale with F sharp *first time*?
- How many times in a row can you repeat this bar correctly? (It's probably a tricky bar but we don't mention that!)
- How many seconds can you hold a long note steadily for?
- How many times in a row can you repeat this four-note figure with perfect control? (Probably a tricky one again.)
- How many different Cs can you play with your eyes closed without hitting a different note?
- How many staccato Ds can you play in one breath?
- How long can you sustain a really steady *crescendo*?

It really does seem to catch pupils' imaginations, so begin building up your own supply. Once pupils get into this entertaining way of working, you'll find that technical issues will be much easier to conquer, especially as pupils regularly try to improve their scores. It can become quite a highlight of their practice activities. And of course it's a painless and entertaining way into attentive repetitive work (see *Practice should include lots of repetition*, page 37).

Another motivational strategy, similar to the above, is creating what we might call *mini-outcomes*. We all love the feel-good factor associated with mastering something, in this case some musical idea or technique. So (perhaps in addition to or instead of the personal best) let's devise *mini-outcomes* on a regular basis. These are different from the *personal best* kind of activity as, rather than relating to more general aspects of technique, they tend to focus on specific areas. Here are some examples of mini-outcomes:

- Can you play/sing the final bar of this piece really beautifully?
- Can you keep your bow straight in this bar?
- Can you perform this section with really vivid dynamics?
- Can you play a G major scale in the left hand with a really crisp *staccato* and musical shape?

Keep them very manageable and easily achievable within one week's practice. Two or three per week is probably quite sufficient. And make sure their achievements are well recognised in the subsequent lesson and that they are well rewarded, perhaps with a (virtual) badge, sticker or points that add up to a prize.

Being positive in our approach to challenges is very important. If set up in the right way, pupils will always enjoy a challenge rather than be put off by it. They will want to meet it, not avoid it. When they do achieve, praise them for their effort, not their ability. In this way we are opening the door ever wider.

Mini outcomes are really very helpful – they give pupils a short-term reason to be doing things as they begin to develop the more mature longer-term reasons like growing a deeper love of music and the understanding of gradual mastery.

Reflecting on practice

From time to time, spend a few minutes with your pupils discussing the positive effects that thoughtful, well-planned and focused practice has had. Reflect with them, once they have mastered a piece or a technique for example, how they actually got there. Why did their practice work? It reinforces a sense of self-confidence and pupils' belief in their own ability to complete tasks and reach goals regularly and successfully.

Do as much as possible

Quality practice does of course (eventually) lead to something approaching perfection. Particularly if enough of it is done and if it's done lovingly and productively. I have mentioned that the major theme of this book is not specifically about *what to do* or *how to do it*, but more about how we program pupils to bring regular practice into their lives in a non-threatening and enjoyable way. As far as *how much* practice is to be done, the general directive is to encourage pupils to practise for as much time as it takes to achieve what they want to achieve. Prescribing a specific practice duration is entirely gratuitous. Parents often like us to do so, but I would rather we spend time explaining to them that a fixed duration will more than likely only lead to clock-watching. And that is simply distracting.

In addition, if pupils regularly fail to meet our recommendations they will build up guilt, leading to anxiety, which ultimately may well cause them to give up. It is much better to allow and encourage pupils to find their own comfortable practice timespan. However, do slip in (frequently but discreetly) the suggestion that *as much as possible* is a worthy ambition!

Occasionally, if you want to increase practice time with pupils, the use of reverse psychology can provide results. We may be able to coax out a little more by restricting it! *'No more than ten minutes a day this week'* will certainly give rise to some curiosity. *'I don't think any more than that would be productive.'* It can definitely work, but it's a strategy best used infrequently.

Read *Mindset* arol Dweck inson) for more his interesting .

For those who see music as a potential career, whether as a performer, teacher or most likely both, practice is going to be the major constituent part of their journey. A lot of it does need to be done. (The general consensus is about ten thousand hours over a period of approximately ten years.) Recent research and thinking now accepts that effort and practice are more important than talent.[14] A little raw talent may be a useful starting point, but if we can inspire our pupils to enjoy practice and do a lot, their chances of success are higher. Ten thousand hours of *enjoyable* practice really will produce spectacular results.

For those who honestly do struggle to find some time, micro-practice is the solution. I hesitate to say this because I don't think the problem *really* exists, but at least it can be a temporary solution as pupils get to grips with the Simultaneous Practice Cycle. For such pupils we can be happy to accept just a few minutes. If we set up their micro-practice in such a way that they are continually making micro-achievements, then confidence and positive feelings will quickly grow and micro-practice will soon develop into something much more significant.

Practising after a lesson, *on the same day*, is very important and should become instinctive as pupils get into the Simultaneous Practice Cycle. It is universally agreed that a greater number of shorter sessions is more productive than fewer longer ones.

Teach pupils to care

Firstly, to care about the quality of their practice. We can help them, for example, to develop the ability to judge how well they are negotiating their way through the Practice Map and to acknowledge and enjoy their achievements. We can also help them to develop a deepening interest in their music and the attendant understanding of how practice plays its part. If they do care, generally they are likely to:

- pay better attention to their work;
- remain focused;
- stay more alert;
- learn more effectively.

There's an interesting scientific reason for this: when we care about things (or equally, get excited) we naturally release the chemical dopamine into our system. Dopamine makes us feel good but it also has the added advantage of causing learning to be more efficient.

So how do we do this? Simply by being genuine in all we do. Caring that we set up practice thoughtfully, caring that we respond to pupils' practice with real interest.

- *'What was the most interesting thing that happened in your practice this week?'*
- *'What was the most interesting thing you achieved in your practice this week?'*
- *'What was the most fun part of this week's practice?'*
- *'Which activities did you most enjoy during your practice?'*
- *'Did you find anything difficult?'*

Look out for what gave your pupils the most pleasure in their practice and make a note of it for future use. If we care, so will they.

Plan for variation in energy levels

Very few of us have consistently uniform energy levels: general feelings of well-being, our mood, the foods we've eaten and sleep patterns all effect energy. Also, growing children will often have less energy. So it follows that the energy levels we have as we begin a practice session will inevitably vary – we need to allow and plan for such variations. Young learners don't need to be told about this in so many words, but if they come back to you complaining that they were too tired to practise or *'didn't feel like doing any'*, then do explain that there are different ways to approach a practice session. Just because their energy levels may be low it doesn't mean practice should be omitted from the schedule!

That means that we do need ready strategies and suggestions for our pupils that cater for both high- *and* low-energy practice sessions.

Each of the *Seven Elements* can be approached with varying degrees of energy. High-energy practice will probably see pupils engaging purposefully with quite a number of them and working through their Practice Map with focus, stopping here and there to think about, explore and develop ideas both old and new. That session may include a certain amount of concentrated technical and repetitive work (more as they advance).

On the other hand, low-energy practice – just as important and useful – may include:

- Playing through pieces (perhaps re-visiting pieces already well known – we often don't encourage enough of this).
- Improvising.
- Consolidating ideas already understood.
- Practising away from the instrument: simply thinking about the music; how to bring out a piece's character; making up a story to fit a piece; thinking about the next high-energy practice!
- Listening to some music, or listening and watching performances on the internet.
- Looking at /studying the score and perhaps some simple analysis of the music.

Actually our energy levels 'micro-fluctuate' quite regularly, and a flow between high- and low-energy practice is probably an ideal for most practice sessions. Once pupils begin to tire and lose concentration, it would be sensible to suggest bringing the practice session to a conclusion in order to end with a strong sense of positive anticipation for the next one.

> The general principles to be drawn from all these strategies relate to the fact that practice revolves around the idea of collaboration. We need to take a lot of trouble to present practice as an attractive activity and discuss it frequently with pupils.

8 What drives and motivates pupils to practise?

> 'The thought of my twin being better at the piano than me ...'
> Louise

Why did *you* practise in your early years of musical development? Was it because you wanted to? Was it to please your parents or because your parents demanded it of you? Was it because you didn't want to be outdone by your musical sister or because you wanted to be like your musical sister? Was it simply because you loved singing or the sound your instrument makes?

There are a great many reasons behind why we find ourselves learning music, some good, some less so. At the extreme end of the spectrum we've all heard terrible stories about children being forced to learn and practise – the results can be spectacular, but at what cost?

It's useful to have some idea of what might be driving our pupils to practise. It will certainly help if they get into difficulties.

Let's get some of the more negative reasons out of the way first.

Some gloomy tales

A very promising pupil was awarded a special scholarship in a school many hours' plane flight from his home. After a while his interest seemed to dwindle and his practice virtually stopped completely. Eventually the question was asked and the answer came as something of a shock: *'My father is not around to beat me'.* Fear of parents can be a strong driving force, but it's about the least satisfactory reason of all. In most cases the results will not lead anywhere helpful. There are some well-known examples of severe parental bullying as a means to drive practice. Hopefully we never will, but if we do ever come to suspect it, or indeed hear about it, we must strongly consider alerting the appropriate authorities.

Practising to please parents may also be of concern. If parents are supporting in all the appropriate *positive* ways, listening to and enjoying their child play through pieces and scales, attending concerts, supplying the necessary finance, the pupil will enjoy and be enthused by the encouragement. But if it is to please a controlling parent (*'If you don't practise properly you're really letting me down'*) then we are into a more difficult situation. We need the child to think about and decide whether they are essentially enjoying their music for their own pleasure and fulfilment. If they are then all is fine (and they will be strengthened by having thought about it). If not, then taking up some other pursuit may be advisable.

Parents who are driving their children to practise so that they can show off their achievements are also a problem. If you get a feeling this might be the case, a solution similar to that suggested above may be necessary.

Occasionally young people are driven to practise by the desire to out-do their peers. It's unlikely that anyone's motivation would be driven solely as a result of this kind of limiting and negative force, but even if there is just a little of this in the mix it will put learners on a road to negativity, fuelling insecurity and potentially provoking even more negative feelings such as jealously.

There's nothing wrong with a bit of healthy competition (the 'real world' creates its fair share), but just practising to out-do others must be gently discouraged as once they've overtaken their friend, there's no more motivation.

Bribery

Extrinsic rewards should be used rarely. I have heard of children being paid to practise (or receive some other kind of 'hard' reward for their efforts). It's not a good idea. If they really don't want to do any, parents need to accept this and try to find alternative routes towards a more positive approach. The occasional and appropriate extrinsic reward though would not be out of place – an outing to a special concert, a lovely book about music, a CD or music download, a smart reed case or a new music-stand, perhaps.

Driven by exams

Many pupils *are* driven to practise, or at least to practise with a lot more focus, when an exam looms. Parents frequently offer the thought that *'Simon only really practises properly when he has an exam coming up'*. There's no denying the truth of this situation in many cases. But if we are convinced that our duty is to make practice a better place to be, then in time we should be able to create an approach where learners really will be able to see the long-term benefits of regular and sustained practising without exams necessarily being the main driving force.[15]

The problem with using exams as the principal driving force is what happens when they stop or become too hard. For pupils who haven't learned to practise for more worthy reasons, the motivation is likely to fade away. And we are all too aware of those pupils for whom learning music and taking exams are virtually synonymous. Is it any surprise that most of these pupils give up at some point, holding the view that learning music is a very stressful experience?

I've occasionally been aware of parents suggesting to their child that *'When you pass your Grade 5, you can give up'*. What sort of motivation is that?

Driven by other short- and medium-term outcomes

Short-term outcomes, such as the regular and stimulating efforts necessary to achieve *personal bests* or *mini-outcomes* (see Chapter 7) are exciting and positive drivers. Medium-term outcomes, such as preparing for a concert or music festival performance, for example, also drive practice in a productive way. If these are managed carefully, practice will always have a sense of positive energy and direction.

or developing
de-ranging,
ginative,
effective
culum, where
ns play their
but don't form
main driving
e, see Chapter
reating the
terplan', of *The
oso Teacher
er Music*).

Practice as a form of pest control

16 As told by Janet Mills in *Instrumental Teaching* (OUP)

It's true! There is a well-known story of a Croatian grandmother who used to practise to deter moths and other bugs from living in her piano.[16] Ten or fifteen minutes of *fortissimo* playing each day and the felts and hammers were safe. An unusual reason for practice perhaps, but I thought it was worthy of inclusion!

To enjoy music with friends

Now we're getting to the most positive reasons for practising. Practice is mostly a solitary occupation. Once pupils have reached a certain level they can begin to enjoy the enormous pleasures of making music with friends. There are so many different possibilities (in both the playing and singing worlds) and once pupils are ready, we need to help them find ways to get involved in group music-making activities. And when they do, they really will begin to reap the rewards of all that practice.

I love my music

Finally we reach the top reason for practice: *'I love my music and I have a strong personal desire to progress'*. Music to our ears. Some children can be deeply inspired by hearing or seeing some music making that will effectively drive them forward for a life-time. It could be anything from a casual performance by a friend, their teacher playing a simple tune or demonstrating what they could do (with a little practice!) or a major performance by a world star (on YouTube, for example). This is why we must continually give pupils (and young children) opportunities to experience music. It's impossible to tell what might ignite the passion, but once ignited ...

Expectancy-value theory (EVT)

There are interesting scientific models to help us understand motivation. 'EVT', developed by psychologist Martin Fishbein, is one such model, and suggests that certain beliefs and values we hold may influence our attitudes towards things. It can be helpful in understanding our more thoughtful pupils' approach to their practice, proposing that pupils are more likely to be driven to practise if:

- They attach some significant importance to being a musician (at whatever level);
- They derive pleasure from their playing or singing;
- They decide that practising will be useful (in some respect) to their future.

To complete the thought, these considerations are set against the 'cost'. *'How much of my time will I have to spend practising and what will my friends think of me if I'm indoors practising when they're outdoors playing football?'*

EVT could make an interesting starting point for a discussion on practice with a more mature pupil.

The practice formula

Finally, an extension of the EVT theory is the rather fun formula for testing whether a pupil may succeed with (for example) a particular piece. The formula is:

Value x Expectation = Motivation

I don't recommend that you use this systematically when considering whether or not to teach a particular piece, but it does have some use in determining how your pupil may get on. This is what it's about …

The **Value** measures how much a pupil wants to learn a certain piece. If they come to you and ask *'Can I learn this piece?'* or *'I really want to learn this piece'*, you know value levels are high. Give their enthusiasm a 'mark' from one to ten. The **Expectation** is how confident the pupil is that they will be able to learn it (they will have their own idea of how 'difficult' it may be and how much work it may take to perfect it). Again give this a mark between one and ten.

So, a pupil really likes a piece (V = 10/10) and thinks *'With a bit of work, which I'm prepared to do as I really like the piece, I shall be able to play it'.* (E = 9/10).

That's 10 x 9 = 90, giving a score of 90 out of 100: the motivation to learn the piece successfully is high. And if this is maintained through successive pieces, we are exponentially moving into a very positive motivational environment.

On the other hand, a pupil may not particularly like the piece (2/10) and thinks it's very difficult, even with hard work (2/10). That's 2 x 2 = 4.

4 out of 100; the motivation to learn *this* piece is very low.

It's not a fool-proof system by any means. With effective Simultaneous Learning we can increase motivation and do wonders for *any* piece. And don't forget that initial reactions often change: with growing familiarity, pupils so often learn to like music about which they were initially sceptical. Although not to be taken too seriously, it's a fun mechanism for making some kind of assessment.

> In summary, knowing what may be the driving force behind our pupils' practice is always helpful in steering them successfully forwards.

9 The parent factor

My father played the violin for a time. His mother had an interesting approach to parenting his practice. She probably thought she was doing the right thing by locking him in a room to practise for half an hour, three or four times a week. He would play his violin for a few minutes before climbing out of the window, playing in the woods behind the house and then climbing back in for another couple of minutes' practice before she came back to let him out.

An enterprising young flute player I know recorded herself playing a scale and a couple of pieces and would replay the recording (night after night) whilst getting on with more appealing pursuits and entertainments. Her parents were never the wiser; in fact they were delighted at the regularity of her practice and rigorously pursued a supportive, non-interference policy that they considered very effective in developing her independence.

Thinking about the parents of my own pupils, I have experienced some quite extreme examples. On the one hand, some sit through virtually every single moment of every single practice session, dictating much of what is to be done, while on the other hand, I have known parents who never involve themselves with their children's practice at all.

Interestingly, both my father and the young flute player (whilst neither reaching very high standards of playing) have always loved and supported music-making. Most of my pupils have done reasonably well, irrespective of whether they went home to exhaustingly ever-present parents or far less-involved, never-present parents.

The fact is that effective parental support and behaviour can come in all sorts of shapes and sizes; it would be impossible to produce a list of hard and fast rules for parents to follow for the maximum positive effect. They are all so different. *But parental support is important.* Very few young musicians will get anywhere without it and this chapter will look at how we can embrace it most effectively.

A cautionary tale

But let's get one form of parental support out of the way quickly. There are many well-known instances in which heavy-handed or excessively ambitious parents have created psychological havoc. Their children may turn into great prodigies but so often at severe cost to their personal well-being. Thankfully it's unlikely we'll meet such extremes, but if we do, there are a number of courses of action we can take. If possible, talk to the parents and try to convince them (in the most reasoned and sympathetic way) that their excessive pushing may well lead to an unhappy end.[17] If they are not prepared to listen, then (depending on the pupil's age and circumstances) try to find an appropriate official in school or elsewhere who can intercede. Failing that, and if the situation becomes unmanageable, offer your apologies and suggest they find another teacher.

17 Suggest they read *Battle Hymn of the Tiger Mother* (Bloomsbury) which relates a very salutary tale.

Most parents, happily, are much more moderate, so let's see how we might help them to play a useful and supportive role in their children's practice.

What parents can do

See section Praise in *The [V]irtuoso Teacher* (Faber Music) p.27.

The two most important things parents need to give their children are *encouragement* and *praise*. When it's due, of course[18], but in as large doses and as often as possible. The main rule to remember is to praise *effort* rather than how wonderful it all sounded. It is now universally recognised that **praising effort** (working hard, perseverance, focus, concentration, commitment, using time well) will motivate much more than **praising ability**. Children who are praised for ability will always be concerned about protecting that label, and become more likely to remain in their comfort zone, avoiding risk-taking and experimentation. When we get into the habit of praising *effort*, experimentation and risk are very much *on* the menu, and there is infinite potential for development.

There are of course other things parents can do such as chauffeuring, paying for things, filling out forms, taking responsibility for instrument maintenance, supporting children through the difficult times and *helping with practice*. All these things should be done in a positive and practical way without becoming over involved or pushing the child for the wrong reasons. Pushing too hard may cause their child to give up, probably the last thing the parent would wish to happen.

Helping with practice

'When my daughter was starting out (aged 6 or 7) I got her to do 20 minutes' practice every morning before school. It was something that 'just happened' and, once a pattern had been established, she did it almost automatically. As she had just had breakfast and was really fresh it was good quality, productive practice. As a consequence her playing ability progressed quite steadily and she could see that regular practice made a real, appreciable difference to what she could do. The progression to the hours of practice that was to follow was therefore an easy and unforced one.'
Peter

If pupils really get into the energy flow generated by the Simultaneous Practice Cycle, then they ought to find their own way into practice on a regular basis. That is our ultimate aim. Of course not all will manage this, and a number may still find the journey into practice quite tough. Making that leap from watching TV, playing computer games or networking with friends may still not happen without some gentle cajoling.

In the early years, a gentle and sensitive push in the direction of practice will probably be required. An important contribution can be to find a suitable time for practice. Parents will know their children's habits and whether they are morning or evening people, for example. Some children will work better when they get into a routine, practising at the same time each day, whilst others may be too involved in other extra-curricular activities to have a set daily practice time, or may simply require a less structured approach.

Should parents sit in on practice? As long as all parties (child, parent and teacher) are happy with the idea, then support in this way may be very helpful. Beginners especially will benefit from this type of parental help and encouragement. As children get older, parental presence becomes less important (and is often undesired), though encouragement and support must never diminish.

There are a number of different opinions on what parents can do in practice sessions. Some writers encourage parents to play a major role in the proceedings. *'Is that the correct fingering?' 'I think you played a wrong note there.' 'That note was a bit flat.' 'Can you get more character in that section?'* Such parents often sit in and take detailed notes during lessons; they assume the role of surrogate teacher. If you and your pupil are happy for this sort of involvement (and it is delivered in an entirely positive manner) then it may be helpful. But parents should remember that it is more important for their child to begin to develop an independence of mind and action, so the sooner they can make themselves surplus to requirements the better.

Other writers on the subject suggest a slightly more hands-off approach with parents just sitting in and gently guiding and reassuring. The hands-on/hands-off decision should be made by the child and may well change from week to week, even from day to day. But if parents are going to sit in, whichever avenue is taken they must never show *any* signs of annoyance, lack of patience or frustration, make inappropriate comments or interrupt when the child is in full flow. Their job should always be to encourage the *child* to determine the overall shape and direction of the practice journey.

In my experience parents feel they need to intervene the most when their children seem vague about what they are to practise. If children really are being taught what to do, and the concept of the Simultaneous Practice Cycle is developing, then there should be minimal uncertainty and parents will have little to worry about.

Outside the practice session there are other valuable ways parents can encourage and support: feeding the personal dossier, getting involved in project work and organising visits to music or instrument museums, concerts and music shops.

Parents as teachers

'I have had to sit down with parents several times and talk about their role as 'fan' and mine as 'teacher'.
Karen

This is a slightly awkward one. For parents who themselves received lessons in younger days, some of whom will have kept their playing up to a good standard, it's very tempting to play the role of the teacher. And then there are those parents who *are* teachers. If you feel inappropriate parental interference may be causing problems the best advice you can give the parent is: only help or advise your child if he or she asks for it, or if things really are going amiss and some sensitive intervention would get things moving forward again. Parents should avoid imposing their own musical or technical ideas on the child and must be *very careful indeed not to indulge in any negative reacting-to-mistakes style comments.* This could seriously undermine the work of the teacher.

I've heard of many cases where parent-teachers create situations that end up in sad disarray. Just one example: a particularly promising cellist school friend of mine (his father was a cello teacher) gave up playing completely. The mixed messages he was receiving from his teacher and his father caused such confusion that he simply couldn't cope.

Of course teaching methods are very different now compared even to a few years ago, especially if we are a Simultaneous Learning teacher. So it is very important to explain to parents how we teach and what we are expecting pupils to do in practice. In such cases, when parents are well-informed, their support can be invaluable.

Knowing the score

Let's give parents a clear expectation of the general shape of a practice session. The Practice Map (or notebook) should be at hand and pupils can explain it to their parents. Parents need to know that good practice will begin with music books *closed,* encouraging their children to practise with their brains and their imaginations turned on! Some posture warm-ups and exercises will get things going, before thoughts turn to the ensuing musical journey and the particular ingredients that will accompany and shape that journey.

The child will probably start with some improvisations on the musical ingredients of the current piece or pieces – something based on the key of the piece or the character of the music, for example. In this way, children are entering into each practice creatively, not just putting the music on the music stand, playing through the piece (complete with numerous mistakes) and then concluding that practice has taken place! That sort of practice may well be akin to what many parents remember if they used to have lessons. But we've moved on: we have to help parents understand what practising in the modern world should sound like.[19]

Perhaps we ht recommend t parents read book or *The uoso Teacher* er Music).

'Have you done your practice?'

This kind of gentle prodding should become less and less necessary as pupils become more tuned-in to practice as a pleasant and natural part of their musical progression. Most young learners would probably not take any offence at such a mild nudge. But if a child has not been practising for a day or two (and there is an exam or performance approaching) the parent may be getting a little concerned. In that case the parent could calmly suggest some practice might be advisable, and conclude *'I'm not angry – I'm just trying to help'.* It may work. But when a nudge starts to evoke guilt then things might get a little more sensitive. *'I'm not angry – but I'm really disappointed'.* Such a comment is unlikely to send a child rushing in the direction of the practice room. Rather than causing irritation, suggest that the parent tries a more thoughtful approach. Here are some options:[20]

20 All these 'responses' are presented as very general suggestions and are not in any way meant to be memorized or used as set scripts! Think of them as generic examples of the type of comment that might be appropriate. Personalities and particular circumstances would naturally have to be taken into account.

> 'I'm getting the feeling that practising is not happening at the moment. Is it because …'

and then explore some of the possibilities found in Chapter 4. This approach, which needs to be spoken in a sympathetic tone, is non-accusatory and shows the child that the parent is sensitive to the problem. Notice how the question swerved around becoming personal. *'I'm getting the feeling that practising is not happening …'* is easier to respond to than the more personal, *'I'm getting the feeling that you're not practising …'* which makes children defensive. Once the problem is identified and sympathized with then it becomes more possible to find a way forward.

> 'I'm troubled that this lack of practice may become a bit of a problem as you have an exam/performance next week. I can see you're feeling unhappy about doing any …'

A respectful and concerned approach that ought to help the child feel confident to talk about the problem. Notice *this lack* rather than *your lack*. Once the child's feelings have been acknowledged then the parent might ask, *'Shall we discuss what you are unhappy about?'* and then try to figure out ways to move forward collaboratively.

> 'I don't want to nag you about practice – let's have a chat and see if we can come up with some positive ideas together …'

The parent is being open, sympathetic and suggesting a practical and helpful way to try to resolve the situation. This might be followed with: *'How about if you did some improvisations or played through some of your favourite pieces today?' 'Would it be useful if I helped you to decide which connections to make?' 'What about more frequent shorter practice sessions or more breaks?'* and so on.

After any of the above approaches, you may like to suggest ending the conversation with the ultimate of unconditional responses:

> 'It would be great if you did get on with some practice, but it's your decision and there will be no consequences on my part if you don't.'

Perhaps this is taking a risk, but not if the child knows that the parent *does* care – and in the right way. If it works, the parent is generating real self-responsibility, and ultimately that is the only way for *genuinely* successful, long-term progress.

Any of these side-door tactics are much more likely to result in finding a way forward rather than being accusatory, annoyed, patronising or tactless, which will probably not.

'I don't want to do any!'

If we are teaching in the Simultaneous Learning manner and using the psychology of the Simultaneous Practice Cycle, this sort of response should become less common! But what can parents do if met with a direct refusal, even in response to some gentle cajoling? The child has in effect thrown down the gauntlet: *'I don't want to practise and what are you going to do about it?'* It's a controlling and attention-seeking tactic. The parent has various options. Getting annoyed will probably only result in a deeper entrenchment. There has to be a measured move towards teaching the child self-responsibility. *'Okay, it's your decision – but is it the right decision?'* The child will have to think about and manage the consequences. The parent may think it useful (gently) to find out why, engaging the child in one or other of the questions above. It may be more complicated if the child is refusing to practise to annoy the parent. A closer look at the deeper motivations behind learning will then be necessary.

If the child is enjoying lessons (and it is of course quite possible to make some progress with no practice at all) then all you need to do is wait for the day to come when the child decides that a little practice might not be such a bad idea after all. Then stand back and watch how it all grows and develops naturally.

All these responses might, of course, also be used by the teacher if we find ourselves having to deal with the situation.

In summary, parents simply need to support sensitively, ensuring practice can take place in as stress-free and relaxed an atmosphere as possible. If teachers have set up practice in a thorough and clearly understandable way, and if pupils are really beginning to absorb the bigger picture through the Simultaneous Practice Cycle, then parents won't have so much to be concerned about. As a result, practice should be both productive and enjoyable.

10 Different goals, different practice?

No two people have *exactly* the same musical aspirations. Some practise to become professional players or singers, for others it is a hobby. Some pupils are very committed and focused, others less so. Some just like to 'play for fun'.

In addition, practice content and the methods employed by a beginner would seem to be very different compared to someone who has been playing for one or two years. For those who have been playing for five or ten years they may seem significantly different again.

I've often had conversations with adults who express a certain resentment that their teachers were not always in tune with their particular musical aspirations. They didn't enjoy what they were told to practise. Too much of it seemed irrelevant to their musical ambitions. They felt that with more sympathetic understanding they may have got much more from their music and might still be playing now.

So does this mean that we should prescribe different ways to practise? Are there different practice procedures for different practice-types?

I know a trombonist who plays in a show band on a cruise ship. He desperately wanted to move into a symphony orchestra, and to this end he would practise for many hours a day. But he didn't know how to listen to himself sufficiently well; he didn't think deeply enough about his playing; he didn't make good connections. It wasn't *effective* practice, so he didn't improve as much as he needed to, and as a result remained much at the same level, and on that cruise ship.

So are there different kinds of practice? I would suggest just two kinds: *effective practice* and *unproductive practice* (or to put it a bit more bluntly, good practice and bad practice).

If we set up our beginners with a really effective approach, that approach will remain broadly the same as they develop. And as they develop even further, perhaps to expert levels (whether as an amateur or a professional), the overall approach *still* remains very much the same.

As musicians become more advanced there will obviously be developments in their practice *technique*: developing players and singers will become more analytical; they will learn to take more trouble over details; they will become increasingly self-reliant, but the fundamental approach (content and method) remains very similar. That's why it is so important to instil effective practice habits from the very beginning. And once a systematic approach has been established it should allow all pupils to develop, each in their own way, as much as they desire.

Virtually everything that emerging, well-rounded musicians do in practice sessions will be drawn and developed from the *Seven Elements* (outlined in Chapter 6):

1 Physical warm-ups

2 Thinking

3 Musical warm-ups

4 Engaging with music through the instrument

5 Listening

6 Projects

7 Developing the personal dossier

It is simply the weight, proportion and intensity given to each of those elements that will define each practice session. Getting that balance right is crucial. This is where perceptive and thoughtful teaching really counts, and will depend on knowing pupils' strengths and weaknesses, their current interests, needs and requirements. Every pupil will require a personalised approach, but within a single and clear scheme made up of our *Seven Elements*.

'I don't do exams, I just play for fun'

There is a tendency for some to attempt to create different types of practice – a case in point would be for those who choose between *taking exams* and *playing for fun*.

I've never really understood this curious dichotomy that many people (often parents) like to express. *'My child doesn't like doing exams, he just plays for fun'*. The fun in 'playing for fun' seems to be of a very limp variety: there's little intention of improvement or progress (making it all rather lifeless and lacking direction). The pupil will probably only play non-challenging pieces; will hardly ever work at technique (no scales for example); will rarely do any aural or theory and will probably do very little practice! The teacher and pupil will probably get bored. Ultimately many pupils who just 'play for fun' will lose interest and give up.

Exams can of course be useful motivators and are best used occasionally as part of an ongoing organic programme. But too often exam syllabuses are used as a curriculum with pupils finding themselves lurching from one exam to another. This is a very stressful kind of teaching and learning that also often results in pupils giving up.

So although there is some difference between these two superficially divergent approaches, they both often move towards the same outcome – the pupil giving up.

If, on the other hand, we take 'fun' learning to mean energetic, purposeful, engaging, stimulating, exciting, worthwhile, meaningful and heartfelt, then we should *always* be 'playing for fun', whether or not we are doing exams. I'd like to see the complete disappearance of ever having to make the unhelpful and pointless decision between 'exams' and 'fun'. We simply get on with our

Simultaneous Learning, where pupils are enjoying themselves and always moving forward in a positive and meaningful way.

Practice phases

As pupils progress through their musical lives they will, however, move in and out of different practice *phases*. No pupil will move through them all, and it will require a little thought as to how we might balance the *Seven Elements* within each. I have identified eight phases:

1 Beginner

2 The developing player/singer

3 The advanced pupil

4 Before and after exams

5 Practising during the holidays

6 The aspiring professional

7 The enthusiastic and advanced player without professional aspirations

8 No longer attending regular lessons but still continuing to play.

The intention in the following thoughts is to identify particular features of each phase that will allow for the most effective progress.

21 Here I mean real beginners, rather than someone who has learnt one instrument for a while and is starting a second.

Beginners[21] generally love their practice and will be very enthusiastic. After a week's practice there will usually be many things to choose from as the starting point for the next lesson, but even if the practice didn't go as you planned, you should still find *something* that pupils did to use and develop as part of the Simultaneous Practice Cycle.

The **developing player** phase begins to emerge when we feel pupils can gradually be given tasks to work out for themselves. Perhaps we prepare just the first half of a piece in the lesson. If the second half contains similar ingredients, the pupil can be sent home to explore and apply what they understand to the remaining half. But we must be confident they will succeed, otherwise we may return to reacting to their mistakes. Carefully, as we notice those pupils who are becoming more self-motivated and able to practise in more depth, we can start to introduce and encourage the use of more sophisticated practice techniques.

More advanced pupils will increasingly need no prior experience of a piece and can be given appropriate new music to take home and learn on their own. We can also begin to sharpen and develop their practice technique. (See also the section below on the *aspiring professional* where you will find many similarities.)

The nature of practice **before and after exams** (at any level) may need some attention. If pupils are taught the Simultaneous Learning way, exam preparation will be well paced and practice (though probably more intense) shouldn't differ significantly from other times. Post-exam practice and lessons are often seen as a time for a major gear change – having a bit of a rest or the now discredited 'playing for fun'. But it's much better to maintain the momentum. Use it as a time for consolidation with perhaps more weighting towards learning a good number of new (not necessarily more difficult) pieces, perhaps further exploration of the instrument (technically and historically) or investigating a composer or a style (baroque music or jazz, for example) in more detail.

For a small number of pupils, **practising and playing during the holidays** continues reasonably regularly, especially those with stronger levels of self-motivation or who are sent on holiday courses of one sort or another. For the rest, practice is often put on hold. But once pupils get into the spirit of the Simultaneous Practice Cycle you may well find that they do indeed begin to practise during the holidays simply as a matter of course. If you are happy to stay in touch, pupils might be invited to make contact on (for example) email.[22] You can ask for updates and make suggestions. Some teachers I know have websites where pupils can log in and provide updates of their practice exploits; the teacher then responds with encouragement, advice and recommendations. Some teachers are also happy to give the occasional lesson during holidays.

Alongside developing their Practice Maps, pupils might like to keep a regular holiday practice diary. Encourage them to record a performance or two for you to watch and offer feedback on. You might use the internet or video links to observe some practice in real time, if the appropriate technology is available.

You may have some senior pupils who could act as practice mentors in the holidays, each being responsible for keeping an eye on a small number of your pupils. Pupils and parents can be encouraged to set up *Practice Parties* – pupils meet up to practise and play together and it all ends up with a bucket of popcorn! If you have the time and inclination you could set up holiday concerts for pupils to play in, trips to professional concerts or perhaps even some busking (having checked out the local bylaws first!). There are a number of useful and fun online musical resources with which pupils can interact, too. Taking all the *Seven Elements* of practice into account, it should be possible to maintain a lot of varied, enjoyable and productive practice during holidays.

In considering practice for the **aspiring professional** we need to help pupils develop a more analytical approach, both to the music they are practising and to themselves; to be more self-reliant and deal with a range of challenges on their own. They also need to do a lot of practice and do it in a *very* mindful, focussed and rigorous way. This is exemplified in what some describe as *purposeful* or *deliberate* practice[23]. Having a clear sense of where each practice session is going, and making that destination always just a little out of reach, will motivate the really ambitious and determined student. Every moment of the session will be filled with clear intentions and precise targets, and those degrees of precision will be ever more resolute – nothing will be left to chance. Developing the *thinking* element of practice is particularly to be encouraged here. Each technical or musical aspect is carefully considered and, in that light, refined, repeated and gradually perfected. Though this is an extreme form of practice it is not in essence different from the practice we have been developing from the beginner onward. The basic principles of thinking, using the imagination and making appropriate connections are still at its heart.

[22] Taking care to follow appropriate child protection guidelines.

Purposeful or *deliberate* practice principally the brainchild of the Swedish scholar K. Anders Ericsson. The concept is especially appropriate to aspiring professionals who want to take their playing to very advanced levels, and is characterised by highly structured, uncompromisingly high-energy practice, driven by very specific goals.

For these pupils we also need to be very aware of the potential stresses and frustrations such practice may generate and help them to manage these intelligently. Teach them about pacing and giving themselves sufficient time to allow both technical and musical growth to happen naturally. There are many **enthusiastic and advanced players without professional aspirations** who may also move into this level of practice and who will require similar support.

Then there are those **no longer attending regular lessons but still continuing to play**, or perhaps parents who would like to re-kindle their playing as their children are now learning. By no longer having regular lessons, those in this phase will have lost the powerful motivational force set up by the Simultaneous Practice Cycle. If they happen to be one of your former pupils, do suggest occasional lessons or encourage regular playing or singing activities: becoming a member of a local orchestra, band, choir or ensemble for example, to help maintain the necessity to practise for the next rehearsal or performance. Also encourage as much listening (virtual or live) as possible so that they know and look forward to the music they are going to practise.

If you are able to help with repertoire choice, always suggest easier and known pieces. Though the challenge of a difficult piece can be fun and inspiring (and would be appropriate at the right time), battling with music that may be technically or musically too hard is ultimately dispiriting and will lead to loss of motivation and eventual termination.

> The seeds of advanced practice are very much sown in the early days. Of course, practice develops and becomes more sophisticated as the beginner moves forward, but the essential content, method and ingredients always remain the same wherever the route leads, be it professional or serious amateur. If pupils can see their practice journey as clear and straightforward they will be less likely to lose their way and give up. Like everything we teach, the development of practice also has a natural forward flow, an organic sense of growth.
>
> If we are to help all pupils enjoy their music to the full, to make the most of their opportunities and reach their individual potentials, we need to consider the importance of establishing this well-defined route and how we adapt it appropriately for each phase as our pupils develop and advance.

11 Do teachers need to practise?

> The legendary cellist Pablo Casals was asked why he continued to practise at the age of 90. *'Because I think I'm making progress',* he replied.

All professional musicians will have their own particular balance between performing and teaching, and this will probably change from term to term, or even from week to week. That balance will no doubt determine how much practice we can fit in. But the fact remains that it is very important that we do practise – and on a regular basis.

Our pupils are often puzzled that their teachers need to practise. *'You're a professional – you don't need to practise!'* And some teachers may think *'I've taught that piece a hundred times – why would I need to practise it?'*

But we do. Even the simplest of pieces. We need to experience how the piece *feels* physically, and think about the kinds of issues our pupils may encounter. We need to have all the ingredients clearly in mind, some of which may only become apparent through actually playing the piece. We need to explore and cultivate appropriate images and metaphors and we need to think about possible opportunities for improvisation. If our muse is available and willing we might even write some useful or entertaining exercises based on the piece or song (or at least develop some ideas for them mentally). By practising pieces we are teaching, as well as other teaching materials we use (sight-reading and scale methods, for example) we will make appropriate connections more spontaneously and effectively. Last but not least, it's very important to experience the sheer pleasure of playing or singing a piece of music from beginning to end.

As you practise the pieces you'll be teaching, try to approach them through the eyes, mind, experience, knowledge and imagination of your pupil. Think about character first. What would appeal? This piece/passage/note is like setting off for a football match, or is it like coming back from a football match and your team has just won – or lost? Maybe it's like waking up and you're still feeling really tired, or it's like floating on a calm lake. Knowing your pupil's interests is invaluable here. The number of possible images and situations are of course infinite, but it's important to think about them before the lesson. If we await inspiration whilst teaching it may not materialise and our imaginations are probably going to be otherwise engaged. Pupils will almost always respond to a vivid, funny or dramatic image. An accented note is far more likely to be brought to life with enthusiasm if the player is trying to give the audience a *shock* or *surprise* rather than just trying to *'play that note louder'*.

Remember to think about *all* of a piece's ingredients, the essential building blocks of a pro-active and energetic lesson. How will we make connections between them? Which connections would be especially pertinent? Which particular ingredients would fit well together to make interesting warm-up exercises? Is there time to write a special and personalised little exercise? Pupils love these and their delight will certainly balance and probably greatly exceed the trouble of writing it. Which ingredients does this particular pupil need to concentrate on? Which ingredients combine well together in some improvisation?

Identify the technical requirements and practise them as your pupils might. What problems might they experience? Factor in their size and muscle development. Perhaps devise appropriate exercises to help. Think: what is it I'm really doing when I do this?

One of the most informative revelations that can emerge from this kind of practice is revealing assumptions we may have about a piece. *'That passage doesn't look awkward ...'* Because we may have taught a piece many times *without playing it*, or without having played it for some time, we can easily miss more subtle complexities. Simple teaching pieces may include deceptively tricky passages that might not become apparent until actually played. This kind of preparation allows us to teach more thoroughly and be more sympathetic!

Practice also gives us the opportunity to explore music we may know well but at a deeper level. Like re-reading a book and discovering hidden depths we hadn't noticed first time around. We might discover a new way to shape a phrase, a new tonal colour, a different fingering, an alternative message. Such work will help us to encourage pupils to do more thinking themselves and extend the range of possibilities. In most cases there is more than one correct solution. I know of a teacher who insists his fingering is always used. He won't begin to entertain any other. That is not the thinking of an effective teacher. Nothing, especially in music, is set in stone.

You don't have to be a great player to be a great teacher – in fact many virtuosi make very poor teachers. They so often don't understand why their pupils can't do it. Sometimes our pupils may be better than we are in certain areas – often technical. This is not grounds for resentment or embarrassment, and it shouldn't cause us to feel bad about ourselves in any way. But teachers do sometimes stop practising for this very reason. Instead, remember that the sum total of our experience will hugely outweigh an occasional pupil's technical prowess. If you feel yourself to be in this place, find some repertoire you used to enjoy – nothing too technically demanding – and re-discover the joys of the music. A little practice like this on a regular basis will help to maintain and in some cases re-ignite that love for actually playing.

The *Six Elements* of practice for teachers

In the same way that we have identified the *Seven Elements* that make up practice for our pupils, there are also different elements that can make up our own practice.

1 *Practising pieces and technique*

We have considered this in detail above, however it is by no means the only activity that constitutes our practice.

2 Information on the internet

There are limitless articles, blogs and websites that are full of interesting, stimulating and up-to-date information on any subject you could think of connected with music education, be it practical, psychological, philosophical, or physiological. There are sites to be found that discuss style, interpretation, technique, instruments – anything and everything. Spend a little time trawling the internet to seek out the new on a regular basis.

3 Listening to music on the internet

In the past, resourceful teachers would make up cassettes or CDs of pieces for their pupils to listen to. It's all so much easier today. We simply guide them to appropriate performances on internet sites. But we can also make lots of use of this resource ourselves. Listen to a new interpretation of an old favourite. Discover some historical performances now made available on some specialist websites. It's a true Aladdin's cave!

4 Thinking and talking about teaching

Full-time teaching can be quite a solitary profession. We may rarely have the chance to get together with other teachers and share ideas and experiences. One very enterprising piano teacher I know arranges a gathering for piano teachers in her area once a month for talking about and sharing teaching ideas and for general socializing. Each member of her club takes turns in offering a venue for the meeting. It's a vibrant and lovely idea, and gives all participants something really important to look forward to on a regular basis.

5 Having a lesson ... attending a masterclass

Teachers should occasionally arrange a lesson themselves – with their old teacher, another musician, a teacher they admire or perhaps even with a friend who teaches a different instrument. Or perhaps take a course in the Alexander Technique. It's good to put ourselves in a learning situation from time to time. Going to a masterclass presented by an interesting musician can be very inspiring – it certainly doesn't have to be on our own instrument or voice. All such experiences are stimulating and energizing.

6 Reading, visiting art galleries, the theatre, cinema ...

Any sort of stimulation to the imagination will do us good! Teachers should always be looking to broaden and re-energize their minds.

There are probably other ideas we can add as part of our suite of practice activities. I see no reason why we shouldn't consider the *Six Elements* as bona fide components in our developing conception of 'practice' in a twenty-first century world. Many teachers feel guilty that they don't always devote regular time to scales, technical exercises and working through pieces. However, the other five elements are central to maintaining a teacher's expertise and should be considered to be of equal status.

12 Practice: the future

If the very foundation of our reason for teaching and playing music is that we love it and take profound pleasure from it … If we see our work as helping others to do the same … If we feel that the world becomes a slightly better place for all our efforts … *Then we don't want our pupils to give up.*

We want them to keep playing music throughout their lives and, by doing so, reap all the wonderful benefits it can bring.

We may have a number of dedicated and self-motivated pupils who practise their pieces, scales and technical exercises with application and focus and with the minimum of pestering. But most don't – and we don't want to lose these pupils. So we must try to re-define practice to fit in with a twenty-first century world. That is not to say that we reject any of the tried and tested methods that have (certainly in a number of cases) successfully produced musicians across all genres, over many decades and indeed centuries. We simply have to put these in a new context, add to them, and develop the whole concept. Too many have rejected music because the practice methods to which they were subjected didn't work for them, causing loss of interest, frustration, and any number of other negative reactions.

The main intention of the ideas described in this book has been to create a process where pupils naturally feel both the need and the desire to practise, as part of an energised, ongoing, organic regime. And I hope I have convinced you that all it will take is a little thought and a little change of approach on our part. Most significantly, we need to take responsibility for our pupils' practice or, conversely, their lack of it! In time, we could indeed influence a truly major change in the way musicians learn.

Lessons and practice: is this really the best formula?

Maybe, sometime in the distant (or perhaps not quite so distant) future we will become sufficiently evolved to lose both the words *practice* and *lesson*. What they stand for will coalesce into one new word to represent a *process* of learning. A process that is organic and ongoing, not split into two discrete units that seem to have only tenuous connections. Lessons and practice should be absolutely connected, because only jointly will they cause really effective learning. Lessons and practice are of equal importance, they are inter-dependent; they lead each other. One day we will develop a new style of education to accommodate this vision.

In the meantime, if you are prepared to take on the Simultaneous Practice Cycle, you should soon see pupils beginning to develop a deeper *awareness* of what they are doing, and as a result, their learning should really begin to flourish.

That awareness is very much at the heart of the matter.

'It's time to do some practice!'

When our pupils hear (or think) these words, we don't want a kind of low-energy, pre-judged, unthinking and mindless response. Instead we need to help them develop some real psychological *control* over their reaction. They need to be taught to be *aware* of this reaction. By teaching our pupils to *understand* the concept that practice is part of a grander scheme to become a better musician, and by encouraging them to take a more collaborative part in the whole process (especially in preparing and planning the Simultaneous Practice Cycle), their response should become mature and positive. Just as they instinctively know that, for example, eating is good, so it becomes with practice.

If someone asks us to do something, or would like us to do something, it is *our* decision as to how we respond to that request, it is *our* decision as to whether we do it willingly and with good grace, or we do it resentfully. If pupils really do 'get it' (the whole practice concept), then their response *will* become more positive; they will want to do it because they see why. And so we will have succeeded: we will have empowered them.

Many writers of books and articles on practice prescribe quite detailed and often fairly rigid instructions in order for effective practice to take place. Whilst no one would disagree with the substance of what they say, a better way to teach someone to become a practice expert is to encourage exploration and experimentation – those two essentials that beginners enjoy so much, at the same time giving plenty of general guidance and advice. Then you can sit back and let each pupil develop the particular practice strategies that work best for them. Pupils *need* to work these things out for themselves. We learn to practise by practising. If we hand it to them on a plate, the ideas are less likely to take root. Set up the perfect mental and physical environment, nourish regularly and watch your pupils grow.

> Practice is a place. By making it a welcoming, safe, engaging, pleasant, positive and fun place to be, we might expect more pupils to accept the invitation and *want* to visit. And if they find it all those things, they are more likely to want to return often. It's very much up to us to take the lead and make the whole practice process something positive and desirable. As a consequence, we have within our grasp the prospect of inspiring ever-increasing numbers of motivated future music-makers.

Also by Paul Harris

Improve your teaching!

Encouraging and inspirational, this is a 'must have' handbook for all instrumental and singing teachers. Outlining Paul Harris' innovative strategy of 'Simultaneous Learning' and packed with comprehensive advice and practical strategies, it offers creative and accessible solutions to the challenges faced in music education.

ISBN 0-571-52534-2

Teaching beginners

This new approach for instrumental and singing teachers emerges from Paul Harris' years of research and experience. By looking at the issues concerning the teaching of beginners, Paul outlines a series of principles, ideas and strategies upon which the best foundations can be laid. The ideas within this book will challenge, affirm and energise your teaching!

ISBN 0-571-53175-X

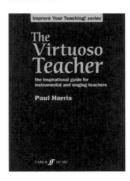

The Virtuoso Teacher

By considering The Virtuoso Teacher and how a teacher might attain virtuoso status, Paul Harris delves into the core issues of being a teacher and the teaching process. This seminal book is an inspirational read for all music teachers, encouraging everyone to consider themselves in a new and uplifted light, and transform their teaching.

ISBN 0-571-53676-X

Group music teaching in practice

This major resource will be invaluable to all teachers involved in group teaching programmes. Packed with practical strategies and advice, it provides a solid foundation for those needing assistance, builds on existing good practice and supports more experienced teachers, moving their teaching on to the next level.

ISBN 0-571-53319-1

To buy Faber Music publications or to find out about the full range of titles available please contact your local music retailer or Faber Music sales enquiries:
Faber Music Ltd, Burnt Mill, Elizabeth Way, Harlow CM20 2HX
Tel: +44 (0) 1279 82 89 82   Fax: +44 (0) 1279 82 89 83
sales@fabermusic.com   fabermusicstore.com